I0468596

Global Economic and Political Insight – 21st Century Challenges

Author: Shabbir H M Tankiwala

Uncertain times are becoming even more uncertain, these are challenging moments for the entire humanity, sort out one problem and another problem rushes in, too many challenges but too few resources available to solve ever existing difficult problems and for dealing with incredibly difficult challenges.

Far too many challenges before us, so many problems, despite so many remarkably intelligent and well-judging minds, yet difficult to find solutions for most of the problems we humans are burdened with.

Crisis is either created by man or crisis is created by nature.

Social problems, healthcare related problems, widespread religious and racial discrimination, ecological imbalance and climatic problems, demographic problems, so many problems and challenges, but, who are responsible for all these problems?

Rising religious intolerance and hatred crimes, steady increase in domestic violence and workplace violence, sexual harassments, forced marriages, forced prostitutions and gruesome incidents of honour killings, women and children particularly vulnerable.

The problems with problem is that one problem creates many more problems.

But the two most devastatingly dangerous problems and arguably the most difficult challenge before humanity is and if we humans fail to find quick solutions than it can potentially or rather most certainly will destroy entire humanity, and these two problems are **Terrorism and Weather (climatic problems)**, the most pressing concerns and biggest challenge before entire humanity in 21st century is wildly increasing religious intolerance, which apparently is giving rise to terrorism and causing social tension and communal disharmony, persistent incidents of brutal killings and violence has evidently ruin peace of mind of billions of people around the world, if self-radicalized individuals and fundamentalists forces whosoever is/are perpetrating crimes and terrorising Masses, frequent terrorist attacks is harming our society and those people who are responsible for killing thousands of innocent people each year around the world. Now, if most people firmly believe that terrorism is most dreadful evil and a menace that's harming and destroying humanity, No friends wait a moment don't blame terrorists alone, terrorism and religious fundamentalism is not foremost dangerous evil as it is thought or believed to be, because even bigger and most frightful and what is particularly causing immense pain to all we humans and which will eventually destroy all of us is the menace of Climate and Weather related problems, yes, imbalanced ecological systems, deteriorating earth's atmosphere, air pollution is damaging and impairing natural environment, so all the impairments and imbalances are causing frequent natural disasters in almost every part and corner of our **Planet Earth**, no region in the world is spared from menacing climatic weather related problems.

Some studies and surveys have discovered that Climatic weather related problems are unquestionably responsible for increase spread of diseases, and for rising poverty and hunger in our world, frequent natural disasters have displaced and have made millions of people homeless in many different countries around the world.

Who is responsible for promoting religious terrorism and for causing environmental problems? The answer, with regards to terrorism, it could perhaps be the selfish self-seeking politicians or the businessmen and perhaps also the religious hierarchy of prominent religions can be or could be blamed for aiding and encouraging terrorists activities and inciting violence. But for deteriorating Climatic conditions, one thing I can say with conviction that, it is without doubt the flawed and erroneous economic policies chiefly of the rich industrialized nations, which are explicitly responsible for damaging earth's atmosphere and causing environmental problems, **extreme Weather problems** like "Flash floods, typhoons, hurricanes, earthquakes, unseasonal rains," all such climatic problems are becoming all too common, frequent natural disasters are damaging properties, destroying agriculture farmland and causing unprecedented financial losses to governments as well to the common people.

Between 2002 and 2015 natural disasters have destroyed livelihood of millions across the globe, ruining millions of acers of farm fields damaging standing crops, spreading dreadful diseases, rendering millions of families and people homeless.

I don't have any data providing precise and accurate figures to quote but it is obvious fact that due to terrorism and natural disasters between 2001 and 2015 hundreds of million people have got displaced and lost their livelihood, besides hundreds of thousands of people have lost their lives.

21st century also marked the start of new millennium as well, but rather sadly 21st century began on far less satisfactory note, right in the beginning of year-2000 the world received first major shock when the inevitable happen, the infamous **DOTCOM bubble burst**, across the globe those avid investors who were heavily invested in shares of companies that were in the business of "Internet, Telecom, Computer-software and Media" suffered massive losses, share value of companies doing business of providing Telecom and Internet services dramatically collapsed and along with it crashed the entire global financial system, stock-market indexes of prominent countries fell sharply reducing influence of many from riches to rags, prices of most companies shares regardless of what business they were in fell sharply and avid investors around the world suffered enormous financial losses, many small and big businesses were literally forced to shut shop between 2000 & 2001 due to weak global economic growth and sombre business sentiments, uncertainty in financial markets and demoralized business sentiments, the global economy than plunged into severe recession, it was not just dotcom burst that the world had to deal with at that time but there were many high profile corporate scams and scandals, the most notable being the **Enron scandal**, Enron Corporation an energy trading company suffered massive lose due to financial irregularities and was declared bankrupt.

But the worst was yet to follow, the world's population suffered for the first time after the end of brutal 2ndWW the most horrific emotional shock, yes here I'm talking about 9/11 (sept-2001) on that miserable day when Islamic terrorists carried out meticulously planned terror attacks on the world's only superpower country "U.S.A," 9/11 terror attacks on U.S soil were by no mean just an ordinary unlawful violence, but there is/was a bigger perspective, it was revival of Islamic resolve to establish **Islamic Caliphate** all over the world, Islamic Sunni jihadi terrorists thru 9/11 terror attacks on U.S soil challenged the entire non-Sunni Muslim communities throughout the world and 9/11 terror attacks gave a strong resounding message to the whole world, that they've arrived and are commencing *Jihad* (Islamic holy war) and it will be fight until finish, now this is what is a serious challenge before entire peace loving world's population, perhaps for the first time in recorded human history, we humans have or are forced to deal with such an excruciating and unsparing crisis in the form of **terrorism and climatic problems**, with regards to Islamic terrorism I would like to point out that after the end of 1st world war, the British and French army forces had substantially neutralized the power of Islamic militancy when they defeated the most ferocious and mighty Ottoman Empire in 1918-19, after remaining subdued for almost 8 decades, the Sunni extremist army once again vigorously staged a comeback and challenging anyone and everyone who is non-Islamic to surrender before them or else suffer the consequences.

Greed becomes Good, Good becomes Bad; in 20th century world witnessed two ferociously fought World Wars, in 2nd half of 20th century as well several bloody wars were fought, Korean war, Vietnam war and Iran – Iraq war which lasted for over 8years, each of these savagely fought wars have had devastating consequences, millions of people lost their lives and millions more suffered acute humiliation and extreme economic hardship but contrary to what people at that time had feared none of these wars sparked the much anticipated 3rd WW.

But as it seems like the worse was reserve for 21st century, what started in January-2011 was initially a peoples movement in Tunisia which soon spill over to other neighbouring countries in the region to *Libya and Egypt*, **Arab Spring Revolution** (or call it **Jasmine revolution**), Arab spring revolution was something similar to 18th century French Revolution, local citizens of Tunisia and Egypt demanding greater freedom, democratic rights and accountability, Arab spring was initially a peaceful peoples movement, local citizens protesting against their respective country's dictatorial regimes, but no sooner had the peaceful Arab spring revolution had started the opportunist Islamic jihadists elements seized the opportunity and crushed the peoples movement and turned the revolutionary process into full blown Islamic Sectarian conflict, the Sunni extremist elements using oppressive measures suppressed the voice of innocent civilians who were seeking and demanding more freedom and justice for themselves in several Muslim ruled African and Arabian countries, since 2011 many Muslim dominated countries in Africa and West-Asia have plunged into deeper social and political crisis, the worst hit and most fiercely affected countries are Yemen, Syria, Libya and Iraq, also countries like Egypt, Tunisia, Nigeria, Kenya as well are among countries which have experienced terrorism, brutal terrorists perpetrating heinous crimes and violence.

Between 2011 and 2015 in several Muslim ruled countries in Arabian region and in Africa well over 400,000 people have lost their life, add couple of more Muslim ruled countries like Pakistan and Afghanistan which as well are equally seriously affected by immense terrorist activities and the count of number of deaths increases by another 20,000 at least, thousands more citizens of these violence affected nations are/were wounded with severe wounds and injuries, so much human blood has shamelessly flowed over the years, the sectarian conflict between Shia and Sunni faction of Islam and other extreme and grotesque acts of graphic violence in many Islamic countries situated in west-Asia and Africa, the terrorists activities gained further momentum since the middle of year-2014. Ever so increasing violence and killings due to civil wars and sectarian conflict between various Islamic factions and groups, with no likely possibility or chance of any kind of compromise or understanding between warring factions of Islam and hopes are fading for finding any amicable lasting peaceful solution to ever so escalating violence and atrocities in Islamic countries and worse still terrorists attacks spreading vigorously to so many other non-Muslim countries as well, therefore by the end of calendar year 2015 assessing the ground realties many political and financial analysts intensely started debating whether if the ongoing civil wars and terrorists perpetrated crimes and violence in Muslim dominated countries "was it or if it is?" an unofficial start of 3rd world war. Whether or not, the magnitude of modern terrorism threat and increase in terror attacks and beheadings of kidnapped hostages of several western countries between 2014 and 2015 can be or can't be construed as unofficial start 3rd WW, but one thing is certain that if and when and if at all, it's a big "**IF,**" the 3rd world war if at all it happens will certainly will be a battle between Islam versus the rest of the world, it potentially will be "**Islam versus the rest' The Third World War.**"

Between 2011 and 2015 due to increased terrorist atrocities and continuing wars in "Syria, Yemen, Iraq and Libya" millions of citizens in these conflict-ridden and violence affected nations have been internally displaced and have lost everything they had of their own, millions of families having lost their homes and businesses, beleaguered citizens are/were forced to flee out of their respective country to seek refuge in other neighbouring countries.

While millions more have or had taken a decision to abandon their own Islamic countries all together and move to other non-Islamic countries to seek protection and shelter, according to some estimates between 2013 and 2015 at least 4.5 million people from various Muslim dominated African and Arabian countries also from Pakistan and Afghanistan have in search for peace and to find shelter have moved to safer zone and for that purpose they are or were compel to make compelling choices and taking undue risk and spending a fortune, fleeing war and poverty migrants left with no alternative had to take a tough decision to cross across the Mediterranean sea, that's how millions of migrants have entered European shore to seek refuge and asylum in prosperous west-European countries, but the small journey of crossing across the sea for these beleaguered migrants to the European shore has not been without the problems, there were horrific tragic incidents of small size overcrowded boat laden with migrants many of the ill-fated boats capsized, resulting in deaths of tens of thousands of migrants by drowning into the sea.

"*This is Real life nightmare* I must say," the political crisis as well as religious and ideological differences between various Islamic and ethnic communities in Muslim dominated countries is the worst thing happening to mankind, the so-called Arab spring revolution has indeed turned into Arab or to say Islamic nightmare.

Humanitarian crisis or humanitarian catastrophe it is arguably worse humanitarian problem since the end of 2nd world war, or in some aspect worse than that was experienced during 2nd world war. Wars and religious violence are wild and callous, most of us know that in past and perhaps even in present times in many countries and in many wars and civil wars official Army, insurgent rebels or terrorists uses **Rape as Weapon of War**, but in Syria's civil war apart from Sexual violence a new method of intimidating enemy forces have emerged, **Starvation as Weapon of War**, local citizens in many villages, towns and cities in Syria are or were being Starved, with intention to pressurize rival enemy forces and to punish supporters of political rivals and opponents, not just in Syria but there are unconfirmed reports suggest that even in some villages and cities in Iraq, Libya and Yemen same pressure tactics are or were used of cutting food and water supply with an intention to suppress opponents and to exert pressure on rival forces. Starvation is not a new weapon but a tactic from medieval times finding modern applications. As a tactic, starvation not only weakens your enemy but also places them under increasing pressure to care for civilians within the besieged site.

But as it is said, that, one problem creates many more problems, the refugee crisis in Europe is clearly humanitarian nightmare, but there is another bigger perspective to understand, the Islamic crisis and civil wars in Muslim dominated countries in west-Asia, Afghanistan, and in Africa has enveloped Europeans as well, the inrush of asylum seekers in Europe mainly from Islamic countries between 2013 and 2015, the sectarian conflict and sharp division among Muslims over their religious issues and factional feud of Islam has put European countries government officials and politicians in bizarre situation and compelled them to deal with rather unimaginable predicament.

As it is that Europe has not fully recovered from the 2008/9 global economic recession, there aren't many or rather it will be safe to assume that there are none, no new business investments particularly in manufacturing sector all over Europe, on economic front not much exciting things happening as of 2014/15 there are No new mega business investments planned for starting any big commercial industrial projects in Europe, unemployment rate as of 2014 in few prominent European countries like "Spain, Italy, Portugal and Greece was well over 15%, unemployment rate is even higher among the youths, so unemployment and underemployment is prevalent all across Europe, rising incidents of crimes, crime rate between 2004 & 2014 has risen exponentially in many key European cities. Keeping in mind abrasive ground realities, hence because of increasing flow of asylum seekers to European countries many thoughtful Rightist leaning individual people in Europe are jittery and resolutely against and unwilling to welcome migrants who are/were migrating from Islamic countries.

So to say, that bitter unending Islamic sectarian and internal religious problems have created problems within the European community as well, Islamic problems and massive flow of large number of refugees and asylum seekers from Muslim dominated countries have had brutally divided Europe into two faction, one faction inside Europe are optimists and have positive feelings for the asylum seekers and supports the idea of allowing migrants in Europe and they argue favourably for granting asylum citing reasons that the migrants from west-Asia based Islamic countries will in long term prove to be an asset and will solve chronic European demographic problems, the optimists are of the view that those migrants entering Europe have skills and talent and their talent can best be utilize for commercial purposes by European businesses, but another faction of Europeans largely consist of rightist activist and Far-Right political parties vehemently opposes any move to accommodate such large flow of millions of migrants from Muslim dominated countries, the rightists elements who opposes allowing entry to migrants are of the opinion that Muslims from Islamic countries only have one talent and that talent is **Combative terror activities and aggression**, the pessimists are arguing that in long term the Muslim refugees once they settle in Europe and consolidate their position and forms their community bases inside Europe, the crafty Islamic folks will destroy millennium old European culture and traditions and will decimate centuries old civilization.

Since the German Government between 2013 & 2015 has granted asylum to over 2 million refugees, and provided them shelter and permission to live and work in Germany, large section of mainstream German society is disgusted and annoyed with their government's **Open Door Refugee Policy**, many Germans are apprehensive because of sudden spurt in Muslim population in their country, as many in Germany fear that in long term it would have profound and devastating social and economic consequences, there is apparent fear in the minds of most Germans and also among many so-called patriotic Europeans as they fear that once the Sunni-Muslim folks establishes base of their community in Germany and France, they (Sunni-Muslims) may potentially float Boko-Haram type of jihadist terrorist outfit and those Sunni jihadists elements would wreck havoc not just in Germany but throughout Europe. Now, whether or not if this is unfounded belief and false apprehension among the Europeans or if it is a genuine concern and fear among Europeans that the Sunni Islamic folks for the purpose of Islamization of Europe would start **nasty urban guerrilla warfare** in European towns and cities and turn Germany and France into Somalia and Libya of Europe, but, another arguably the most pressing concern among the European community is that Islamic jihadists may capture young beautiful European girls and women and force them to marry jihadists or make them sex slave.

So there are/were conflicting views and split opinions among the Europeans with regards to granting asylum and to give permission to mostly Sunni-Muslim migrants from Islamic countries to settle in different prosperous European counties and earn their livelihood and their young children gets best education, so that

Muslim community folks like other Europeans enjoy every basic fundamental and civil rights as per the European laws.

What has/had further harmed the Muslim community cause are/were the frequent terror attacks by the jihadi Islamist Sunni terrorists, couple of terror attacks in Tunisia killing many European tourists, couple of massive terror attacks in France and few minor but intense terror attacks in several other European countries between 2014/15, and also abrupt behaviour of young Muslim men allegedly found guilty of having Physically Abused and Sexually Assaulted young White European Women in German city of **Cologne** on New year's Eve, Muslims involvement in such barbaric crimes sparked major anti-Islam sentiments all over Europe and also in north-America,

Between 2013 & 2015, Series of terror attacks in many different countries around the world killing thousands of innocent people, --- and beheadings of several European and American nationals allegedly in Syria by inhuman Islamist Sunni jihadists, such inhumane crimes against humanity perpetrated by Muslims has made Muslim position untenable, Muslims have become unpopular and whole Islamic community particularly the Sunni-Muslims have been embarrassed and stigmatized by the acts and actions of their community members, also I would like to point out "all jihadi terrorists groups owes allegiance to Sunni Islam."

Spate of terrorist attacks in several European countries and rising incidents of crimes in European towns and cities has taken its toll on Europe's once thriving Tourism industry, millions of Chinese citizens are worth millions of U.S Dollars and have incredibly high spending and purchasing power, once Europe was most preferred holiday destination for the Chinese, millions of Chinese folks use to travel to Europe and U.S each year to spend their holidays, but sharp decline (devaluation of Yuan) in value of China's currency against major international currencies particularly the "Euro and U.S-Dollar" increases the cost of holidaying in Europe but that's only one small part of the reason, more important reason is safety concern among China's nationals, frequent terror attacks and high degree of crime rate in Europe forced many Rich Chinese to alter their annual holiday travel plans, so since middle of 2015 many Chinese did a rethink and allegedly cancelled any plan if at all they had of spending their holidays in Europe or even in other troubled mainstream tourist destination of the world which apparently are not too far away from shores of Europe countries like Turkey, Egypt and Tunisia, and instead Chinese opts to travel to more safer countries in Asia. While supper rich Chinese prefers to travel to Japan, New Zealand and Australia to spend holidays, the middle-income folks from China prefers to travel to countries like Thailand, Dubai, Indonesia and South-Africa to spend leisure holidays, thereby massively hurting business interest of Europeans as well also of the troubled Islamic countries like "Tunisia, Egypt and Turkey" which as well are considered unsafe due to increase terror attacks and rampant fear of Sunni jihadist terrorists. But not only the Chinese even the rich and wealthy Asian Muslims as well instead of Europe they prefer to spend their leisure holidays in countries like Malaysia, Thailand, Singapore and or in Dubai. So if Europe and Egypt are losing business others like Australia and Malaysia etc are gaining, as there is a saying, "One man's misfortune is an opportunity for another man."

If we are discussing 21st century humanitarian crisis and of Europe's political and economic crisis then it is also important for us to understand little bit of past Europe's history as well, here I would like to share an interesting Article title **"Political Situation in Europe on the Eve of French Revolution,"** "On the eve of the French Revolution the political situation in Europe was remarkably simple. The Continent was dominated by five great powers: Britain, France, Austria, Russia, and Prussia. Their neighbors – Spain, Sweden, and Turkey – had all once enjoyed periods of economic, military, or naval greatness, but by the end of the 18th century had slipped into the ranks of the lesser powers. Most of western Germany remained fragmented into hundreds of minor principalities, ecclesiastical cities, and minor states contained within the Holy Roman Empire. Italy, similarly, contained a number of small kingdoms, some independent and others controlled by Austria. Europe was overwhelmingly agrarian and feudal, particularly in the east, with monarchs ruling absolutely within their domains. Britain was a somewhat different case: though the vast majority of her people were disenfranchised, the monarchy ruled under constitutional constraints. The nation's prosperity was based not on agriculture but on trade. The process of industrialization, though still in its infancy, was well under way.

A generation before the French Revolution, Prussia, under the ruling house of Hohenzollern, had established herself as Europe's newest great power, having won a series of costly and exhausting wars in which she had taken on and defeated practically every major state on the Continent. Frederick the Great had inherited from his father, Frederick William (1713-40), a highly militarized, extremely efficient state where the landed aristocracy and king enjoyed a close relationship. The aristocracy were freeholders of their land and, in effect, over their peasants as well. In return, the crown taxed the nation heavily in order to maintain a standing army proportionally much larger than that of any other European state. Frederick used that army aggressively: he invaded Austrian Silesia in 1740, and thus began the War of the Austrian Succession (1740-48). This was followed by the Seven Years' War (1756-63) (see Osprey Essential Histories, The Seven Years' War, by Daniel Marston) in which Prussia used her formidable army for the glory of the nation and to consolidate her territorial gains, generally at the expense of Austria. During the Seven Years' War Frederick fought the greatest coalition ever seen in Europe – Austria, France, Russia, Sweden, and most of the German states of the Holy Roman Empire – and survived intact. It was the hard-fought bloody encounters of this war that confirmed for Prussia her place among the Great Powers.

The Russian Empire covered a vast stretch of territory containing at the turn of the century about 48 million subjects, over half of whom were serfs tied to the land. The autocratic Romanov dynasty had ruled since the early 17th century. Russia's military reputation had been won under Peter the Great, who had defeated the Swedes in the Great Northern War (1700-21). Although Russia had briefly fought Prussia in the later years of the Seven Years' War, her territorial gains were made at Polish and Turkish expense during the reign of Catherine the Great (1762-96), particularly during the First Partition of Poland in 1772 and in the annexation of the Crimea, an Ottoman possession, in 1783. Russia fought simultaneous conflicts with Sweden (1788-90) and, in alliance with Austria, Turkey (1787-92). She was ultimately successful in both of these conflicts. When the French Revolutionary Wars began, Catherine the Great remained neutral and she died four years later in 1796 without having challenged the Revolution. That task was left to her son and successor, Paul I, who would finally face France during the War of the Second Coalition (1798-1802). Paul was known for his mental instability and obsession with military matters and was assassinated in 1801.

George III, who had presided over the somewhat different and more constitutional monarchy of Britain since 1760, proved to be one of the French Revolution's most implacable opponents. Political power rested with Parliament and the Prime Minister. William Pitt the Younger had attained office in 1783 with a loyal following in the House of Commons and the support of the crown. Though small by continental standards – with a population of fewer than 10 million – Britain was the world's most prosperous nation. Her wealth was based on thriving trade with Europe and her exclusive access to a vast empire which, in addition to Canada and, above all, India, included newly acquired territories in Australia and many of the bountiful "sugar islands" of the West Indies. As international trade was the basis of the rapidly increasing national wealth, the protection of trade was paramount. Britain's unrivalled merchant fleet, which exceeded 10,000 vessels, could confidently rely on the power of the Royal Navy for its protection. Although agriculture was still important – accounting for one-third of the national product – Britain was the birthplace of the recent phenomenon of industrialization, and its growing manufacturing capacity played a major role in stimulating a booming economy. Britain and France were long-standing enemies, having fought one another regularly over the past century and on opposite sides in nearly every conflict in which the two countries were engaged since the Middle Ages."........

This are defining moments, I call it evolving situation! Conflicting views and varied opinions, selfish motives and purposes, internal rift and confusion among European politicians over drafting more acceptable "European immigration policy," the humanitarian crisis is/was far more severe in 2015/16 than it was in 1945/46 after the end of 2nd WW.

Terrorism, the Islamic jihadists elements, growing religious intolerance, deteriorating global weather and climatic conditions, and last but not least Cyber hackers or cyber terrorists call them whatever you like to call, but Cyber hackers as well are causing immense harm and pain, so these are some of the main 21st Century Challenges, how we humans are going to deal with such excruciating challenges and how we'll overcome difficult situations, well only time alone will tell.

It is not an argument to prove as in "Who is right or wrong' but through discussion we need to understand, as to, What is right or wrong."

But if terrorism is bad enough evil and devastatingly harming humanity, deteriorating climatic weather condition is much more troublesome menace, if we take into account the loss we humans have suffered due to frequent natural disasters, the loss of lives and financial losses that we humans have suffered is incredibly high, between 2001 and 2015 because of Warming oceans and changing climate has resulted in causing extreme weather patterns, all combination of factors are destroying world's ecological system and as a result of which frequent natural disasters keeps occurring across the world, millions of people have lost their life and have suffered trillions of U.S dollar worth of business loss and damages to properties and agriculture farmland. The most notable among all natural disasters thus far in 21st century was the **high tsunami waves** that occurred in Indonesia and which also profoundly affected countries closer to it, primarily it was Indonesia that was most brutally affected that's because Indonesia was the first country to be affected by the massive earthquake in Indian ocean which caused high tsunami waves, the worst hit countries were Indonesia, Thailand, Sri Lanka and India, it happened on 26-12-2004 and over 230,000 people are reported to have died.

Indonesia and Philippine perhaps are most prone to natural disaster, but, even rich and developed countries as well are not spared, in fact the developed countries are experiencing some of the most horrific and extremely rough climate, increasing occurrence of severe weather, extreme weather events are a consequence of climate change and are becoming more frequent powerful and erratic, countries such as China, U.S, Britain, west-European countries and of course Japan, all these rich industrialized countries have suffered extremely high loss of business and properties and massive loss of lives of their citizens. Every continent has been affected, from one of the world's strongest storms hitting the Philippines and the widest tornado ever seen in the United States, to extreme droughts gripping central Africa, Brazil and Australia and a series of massive floods in Pakistan.

But then it is the rich industrialized nations who are in first place responsible for creating or causing irreparable damage to the world's atmosphere, it is their flawed and faulty economic policies that has or is destroying Planet earth's environment and ecological system and have put at risk lives of entire global population.

Not as much the terrorism but it is the climatic weather related problems which apparently is principle reason for economic uncertainty and ever rising hunger and poverty in the world

So, be it terrorism or climatic problems, both these crisis are man created, humans own created problems which are easy to solve yet no one wants to solve it, yes, it is we humans ourselves are incontrovertibly responsible for all our woes.

It is of paramount concern and desire of each human to have roof over top of his/her head, to have a home that we can call our own home, there are people in our world who are unfortunately born into poverty and are homeless since the time of their birth, but so unfortunate are those folks who were living a blissful and happy life and had everything including beautiful home, those people who were living fully satisfied life but one day tragedy struck and for no fault of theirs they lost everything they had of their own, here I'm referring to those hapless people who have lost home, livelihood and seen their families disintegrated, yes, this is what happens, or this is what has actually happened to hundreds of millions of people who are seriously impacted because of devastating natural disasters that have destroyed lives and livelihood of so many people around the world and of those people whose happiness is or was smashed and misery brought into their life by political instability and or because of wars or civil wars in their country or when terrorists and criminal gangs ransacked their towns and cities.

So there are millions of homeless who are displaced or are in homeless situation, it is because either the city or the country they use to live in has plunged into sectarian unrest or communal violence or plunged into deadly civil war or the criminal gangs and terrorists groups have captured the town where they use to live in and have destabilized their country, or if the country or city they use to live in was struck by natural disaster that ruin their home, killed their near and dear ones and decimated their source of income.

According to some estimates which suggest that as of year 2014 there are over 200 million people who are homeless, however this figures could be even higher, because getting accurate information with regards to global homelessness in extremely challenging, also definition of homelessness varies from country to country, there are also factors like hidden homelessness those folks who are residing in inadequate settlements such as slums, according to estimates close to 200 million people are literally homeless, they have no shelter they sleep on pavements, in doorways or under the bridge, or they sleep in public places like railway station or at bus station.

The problem of homelessness in not as if it is limited to 3rd world or under develop countries, as of 2014 there were as many as 2.5 million homeless in otherwise prosperous European union countries and nearly 700,000 people homeless in U.S.A on any giving night spending nights sleeping in public place or in emergency shelter.

If anyone wonders as in, why homelessness in so pervasive worldwide? There are number of reasons, causes of homelessness varies, most common basic economic level homelessness is because of poverty and unemployment also billion plus people in different countries are underemployed so such individual people can't afford decent housing, expensive and unaffordable housing ---- millions of poor can't afford to buy home because they simply do not have enough money to buy even ordinary dwelling, high level of corruption in higher offices of power and flawed economic policies further compounds matters, because in many countries the poor do not carry adequate political weight, hence governments in many countries do not feel political pressure to take corrective measures to improve housing and to implement other anti-poverty programmes for removal of poverty.

The social sector welfare and improvement has been left behind, what the world's population need is **Not** solid economic reforms but purposeful and comprehensive **Social sector reforms**, which will ultimately improve comfort level of people and will make our towns and cities better place to live in, Human minds has creativity. When citizens and government bureaucracy get together then by discussions and by using their creativity most problems can be solved. All that is required is to create a human mechanism or apparatus which can liberate the potential creativity.

The problem is that in most of the 3rd world and developing countries the infrastructure (water, electricity supply, roads, drainage, sewers, schools, hospitals etc.) has not improved or increased at the same rate as the increase in the population. Consequently, residents of cities are facing the regular nightmare for lack of water and electricity, bad roads etc.

According to one of the reports prepared by Unicef, nearly 40% of the world's population lacks access to proper toilets. According to some estimates 6 in 10 Africans remain without access to proper toilet, poor sanitation threatens public health.

Sanitation is not a dirty word, sanitation matters, "Sanitation is a cornerstone of public health and wellbeing," sanitation has seriously lagged behind time, the absence of sanitation has severely impacted the health and social development of most people around the world. Sanitation facility provides a person safety and dignity.

Millions of girl child around the world are withdrawn from schools and colleges once they reach puberty, particularly hard hit are girls from Indian sub-continent countries like India, Pakistan, Bangladesh and Afghanistan also girl child in African and south-American countries are most impacted, because the schools and colleges in most of these countries are not equipped to provide clean water and soaps to young girls to wash themselves and to maintain high degree of hygiene.

Article title **"A bad climate for development"** has written; "The poor are more vulnerable than the rich for several reasons. Flimsy housing, poor health and inadequate health care mean that natural disasters of all kinds hurt them more. When Hurricane Mitch swept through Honduras in 1998, for example, poor households lost 15-20% of their assets but the rich lost only 3%.

Global warming aggravates that. It also increases the chances of catching the life-threatening diseases that are more prevalent in poorer countries. In many places cities have been built just above a so-called "malaria line", above which malaria-bearing mosquitoes cannot survive (Nairobi is one example). Warmer weather allows the bugs to move into previously unaffected altitudes, spreading a disease that is already the biggest killer in Africa. By 2030 climate change may expose 90m more people to malaria in Africa alone. Similarly, meningitis outbreaks in Africa are strongly correlated with drought. Both are likely to increase. Diarrhoea is forecast to rise 5% by 2020 in poor countries because of climate change. Dengue fever has been expanding its range: its incidence doubled in parts of the Americas between 1995-97 and 2005-07. On one estimate, 60% of the world's population will be exposed to the disease by 2070."............

The desire to live a long, happy and healthy life is something we all desire. Several factors come into play while determining whether a country is suitable for living a valued and healthy life, every country is measured by its human development index and if there is political and social stability.

Structural discrimination prevents many of us to live a wealthy and healthy life, it is therefore necessary for every country to have well entrenched civic and civil infrastructure and public infrastructure for utmost benefit of their citizens.

It makes us feel proud to live in a country which has efficient political governing system and up-to-date public infrastructure, it is extremely troublesome and painful to be citizen of a country that has appallingly poor civil and public infrastructure and inefficient political system. India and China are two of the most populous countries in the world, while China is over invested and have excessive public infrastructure, in stark contrast the story is different in it is neighbouring country India, India has severe infrastructure deficiency and one of the worst civil and public infrastructure in the world.

There are countries in the world which are naturally blessed with vast natural resources, resource rich countries treats available natural resources in their country like mulching cow, many resource dependent countries largely survive on single source of income which it derives from selling domestically available resources like minerals or petroleum oil in international markets and earns foreign exchange. Countries for example **Venezuela** which is overwhelmingly dependant on income it earns from selling petroleum crude oil, or another south-American country **Chile** which relies heavily on income it generates from selling copper to international buyers, similarly countries like Brazil and Australia which are largely commodity producing and exporting economies, then there are countries like Saudi Arabia, Iraq and Russia they all vehemently rely on money they earn from selling petroleum crude oil and gas in international markets.

The fortune of resource dependent nations are intrinsically linked to the price movements of various commodities in international commodity markets, so when there is buoyancy in commodity markets and when prices of various commodities are trading higher, when prices of Base Metals, precious metals and petroleum oil and gas are firm and trades and higher levels, higher prices of commodities are blessing for countries that are principle producers and exporters of commodities, but, when the prices begins to fall and commodity markets suffers sharp decline and prices of various commodities starts trading at unprecedented lower levels then it begins to severely harm resource dependent nations, it happens this way, when prices of commodities are higher, so obviously the producing nations earns lots of money and when natural resource rich nations earns lot of money they as well generously and lavishly spend money, governments gives big incentives and benefits to government employees as well generously spends money on public healthcare and welfare schemes and resorts to other populist measures to help its citizens. Now, when due to sharp decrease in prices of commodities or otherwise for any other reason/reasons if government revenue department of any particular country earns lower tax revenue and if corporates aren't performing well and due to demand recession for consumer products and services the companies are reporting lower profits or even suffering loses, in which case government may react by cutting Public expenditure and Capital spending, hence government will have to resort to cost saving measures and to achieve that target, will have to withdraw all or at least some of the benefits that it provides government employees and to its citizens and will have to further reduce expenditure by cutting or reducing subsidies that it provides to farmers or to the industrial sector.

The resource dependant countries citizens fortune distinctively and intrinsically are linked to price movements the resource (hard or soft commodity) their country produces, higher prices of commodity means higher income from Royalty and various taxes hence it will help their government administration increase Public expenditure as well help increase Capital spending which in turn will help the citizens as it will create better job and business opportunities therefore will improve their lifestyles and hence increase their purchasing and spending power, and when in times of misery when the prices of commodities declines and declines sharply the country's currency as well will trade lower in value against peer currencies, so, uncertainty in country's Forex markets and Capital markets will force their government to restrict itself of any wasteful expenditure therefore curb their spending which apparently directly impacts the citizens and tremendously lowers their spending power that's because massively lower government spending will harm businesses therefore will severely impact employment growth, here it compels us to think, as to, how risky it can be for countries to pin their hopes for economic growth exclusively upon exporting commodities, such as oil and metals, whose global prices are highly unpredictable.

Regardless of what the actual reality is, whether we talk about resource rich nations or commodity importing nations, when so ever the governments receipts and tax revenue drops, this most likely happens when the businesses aren't performing well, businesses not performing well could be perhaps because of initial over production which may cause higher inventories of industrial goods and consumer products, which apparently compels manufacturing industries to produce less because of already existing unsold large inventories and when industries lowers there production obviously they need less employees so jobs are loss and redundancy rises when people aren't earning more and if there is joblessness there will be further drop in demand for consumer products, because of lower tax revenue collections the governments have to then cut capital expenditure and if left with no other option than have to hike taxes further and levy higher duties and sharply reduce Planned expenditures on social sector, healthcare and public infrastructure, so when governments of several countries at the same time are compel to reduce spending and under extraordinary circumstances have to enormously lower spending on social sector infrastructure that is what creates **Global Economic Recession**, because of no new investments in social sector infrastructure and public infrastructure, or no upgradation and modernization of existing infrastructure it only creates many more social and political problems, because local citizens starts feeling discomfort and disenchanted with their respective country government administration, dissatisfaction among large civilian population could emotionally provoke and make local citizens restless of that or those particular country/countries which are hardest hit by economic downturn, so extreme economic problems gives rise to civilian unrest.

In all economies, an efficient and sustainable reduction in the fiscal deficit requires a sound mix of revenue and expenditure policies. A government facing the need to reduce speedily the fiscal deficit may at times find it difficult or impossible to raise the level of revenue in the short run. Increasing the productivity of public programs can provide a viable option that will release resources to reduce the deficit or to expand other critical public programs. Moreover, the government may want to reduce the size of the public sector and the level of public expenditure over time because the public sector is engaged in activities that can be carried out more efficiently by the private sector. Even without a major fiscal imbalance or a large public sector, some categories of public expenditure may be so inefficient that improving efficiency could release resources to expand other critical public programs or to reduce the deficit.

Peace, progress and prosperity in any country depends on variety and combination of factors, perfect balance needs to be worked out between demand and supply of goods and services, when unmindful governments to gain popularity and to give artificial boost to their country's economic growth and to inflate companies Share prices on Stock-markets, desperate governments designs economic policies to boost economic growth, wherein they recklessly forces industries to produce more goods and encourages their citizens to generously over spend money on buying consumer products and other fancy items, and for the convenience of industrial sector to manufacture and to produce more goods and for common-people to spend more money, the Economic policy planners and Central bankers of many countries in more recent times have found one and only measure which is to first "lower the Prime lending Bank's interest rate to Zero %," and if that's not enough create more and more cash liquidity into the banking system, Printing unprecedented amount of currency notes and flooding the Banking system with vast amount of cash for the Banks to have extraordinarily excessive amount of cash (currency) available in their system to lend it to the borrowers, so that businesses and manufacturing industries can borrow more money from lending institutions literally at free of cost at near zero% interest rate, and so does it facilitates to the common-people as well to borrow easily available cheap cash-credit or to say inexpensive loans to buy and spend more money on purchasing consumer durable items and also for spending money on exotic vacations at sumptuous locales and with inexpensive loans available people can freely buy wanted or unwanted fancy luxury items, this is how Institutions using inorganic methods spurs economic growth. **"Institutions have Institutionalized corruption,"** but such economic growth can't sustain for long and one day the bubble inevitably burst and creates unprecedented financial as well as humanitarian crisis, Credit cards encourage people to spend money they do not have. Debts can build up and leave people in real financial difficulties. When people cannot pay their debts back, everyone suffers: those in debt may lose their homes, the banks lose money, and the whole economy suffers.

In simple terms to understand that Base-Metals (aluminium, copper, zinc, nickel), minerals and petroleum oil and gas are basic raw material for manufacturing industrial goods and consumer durable products and are widely used in commercial and industrial applications, call it Quantitative easing or Economic stimulus package, Printing currency notes to create excessive cash liquidity, large amount of cash availability entices greedy Capitalist bankers to invest and to lend more money to mineral mining and oil and gas exploration companies, unrestrained mining and exploration activities brutally harms natural environment and destroys ecological system, which apparently causes global warming and climatic problems, and this is what has put humanity on the brink of becoming extinct.

I would like to share excerpts from an interesting article "**Global Economic Downturn: A Crisis of Political Economy,**" "As we all know, the origin of the 2008/9 financial crisis was the **subprime mortgage meltdown in the United States**. To be more precise, it originated in a financial system generating paper assets whose value depended on the price of housing. It assumed that the price of homes would always rise and, at the very least, if the price fluctuated the value of the paper could still be determined. Neither proved to be true. The price of housing declined and, worse, the value of the paper assets became indeterminate. This placed the entire American financial system in a state of gridlock and **the crisis spilled over into Europe**, where many financial institutions had purchased the paper as well.

There was a crisis of confidence in the financial system and a crisis of confidence in the political system. The U.S. government's actions in September 2008 were designed first to deal with the failures of the financial system. Many expected this would be followed by dealing with the failures of the financial elite, but this is perceived not to have happened. Indeed, the perception is that having spent large sums of money to stabilize the financial system, the political elite allowed the financial elite to manage the system to its benefit.

This generated the second crisis — the crisis of the political elite. The Tea Party movement emerged in part as critics of the political elite, focusing on the measures taken to stabilize the system and arguing that it had created a new financial crisis, this time in excessive sovereign debt. The Tea Party's perception was extreme, but the idea was that the political elite had solved the financial problem both by generating massive debt and by accumulating excessive state power. Its argument was that the political elite used the financial crisis to dramatically increase the power of the state (health care reform was the poster child for this) while mismanaging the financial system through excessive sovereign debt.

The Crisis in Europe

The sovereign debt question also created both a financial crisis and then a political crisis in Europe. While the American financial crisis certainly affected Europe, the European political crisis was deepened by the resulting recession. There had long been a minority in Europe who felt that the European Union had been constructed either to support the financial elite at the expense of the broader population or to strengthen Northern Europe, particularly France and Germany, at the expense of the periphery — or both. What had been a minority view was strengthened by the recession.

The European crisis paralleled the American crisis in that financial institutions were bailed out. But the deeper crisis was that Europe did not act as a single unit to deal with all European banks but instead worked on a national basis, with each nation focused on its own banks and the European Central Bank seeming to favor Northern Europe in general and Germany in particular. This became the theme particularly when the recession generated disproportionate crises in peripheral countries like Greece.

There are two narratives to the story. One is the German version, which has become the common explanation. It holds that Greece wound up in a sovereign debt crisis because of the irresponsibility of the Greek government in maintaining social welfare programs in excess of what it could fund, and now the Greeks were expecting others, particularly the Germans, to bail them out."............

Undemocratic, unprincipled and unethical measures taken and methods adopted to boost their country's economic growth as well to add impetus to global economic growth, by frequently implementing economic stimulus package wherein as a first step is to reduce short term commercial borrowing interest rate to Zero% and if that's not enough than start printing unlimited amount of cash-currency notes for indefinite period of time, such measures have become all to frequent norms and are chiefly executed by leading industrialized nations Central bankers, creating massive cash liquidity in banking system, such unnatural measures to augment industrial growth and for the purpose to improve public spending, substantially reducing cost of borrowing for the businesses and for citizens of their country to as low as it possibly could go or in some case businesses can borrow money from banks and other lending financial institutions literally are Zero % interest rate, so all these for the sake to create demand for new Homes, automobiles, consumer products and durable items.

High levels of public debt also call into question whether the debt will be repaid in full. That can lead to a higher risk premium, and that's associated with higher long-term real interest rates, which in turn has negative implications for investment as well as for consumption of durables and other interest-sensitive sectors, such as housing. However, the evidence shows that soaring government debt has resulted in slower economic growth. It also suggests that we should be very wary of arguments for any further short-term fiscal stimulus, as the long-term secular costs of high debt service could easily outweigh any potential short-term benefits. When government debt grows, private investment shrinks, lowering future growth and future wages.

If we need to get more money into the economy – for example, during a recession – then we have to go further into debt to the banks. This is why the government is desperate to get banks lending again: if banks start lending more, they'll create more new money in the process, and the people who borrowed will spend this new money.

But if the financial crisis are caused by people having too much debt, how can the solution be for people to take on more debt?

So when lots of people try to pay down their debts at the same time, money disappears from the economy. As a result of there being less money and less new lending spending slows down. When this happens, it's like draining the oil from the engine of a car: pretty soon, everything stops working.

This means that **it's almost impossible to reduce our debts without causing a recession.** And you personally can only pay off your debts using money that was created when someone else went into debt. This creates a debt trap, where over time the level of personal debt in the economy has to keep growing.

The Fed (U.S Central Bank) used a dual-track response to the recession and financial crisis. It adopted some unconventional policies, such as the purchase of $1.25 trillion of mortgage-backed securities. And the FOMC reduced its interest rate target to near zero in December 2008 and indicated its intent to maintain a low interest rate environment for an "extended period." Recently, some economists have begun to discuss the costs and benefits of maintaining extremely low short-term interest rates for an extended period.

As borrowing increases, the government have to pay higher interest rate payments to those who hold bonds (lend government money). In some circumstances, higher borrowing can push up interest rates because markets are nervous about government's ability to repay. This means they have to pay even higher interest rate costs. Currently, the UK pays approximately £43bn in interest payments.

It is rare for government borrowing to cause inflation. But, the combination of quantitative easing and very high levels of borrowing make inflation more likely.

If markets fail to buy enough gilts to finance the deficit, the deficit can always be financed through 'monetization'. i.e. creating money. This creation of money creates inflation, reduces the value of exchange rate and makes foreign investors unwilling to hold debt. So far quantitative easing has not caused inflation because of the falling velocity of circulation. But, if the economy was close to full capacity, printing money to 'monetize the debt' would lead to inflation. In the case of Zimbabwe this could lead to hyperinflation.

Now many among us believe and there is a general popular perception that if Central Banks keeps aiding industries and businesses by printing cash-currency notes it will help power economic growth and create massive demand for durables and consumer products, but do a reality check and you'll find that economic stimulus packages only creates bubble and in long term severely harms the economic growth and creates bigger social and political problems, thus far (as of 2015) in 21st century the world has witness two Boom and Bust cycle in Commodity markets, first between 2006/7 when prices of commodities hit record high levels particularly the price of crude oil which at one point traded at historic high levels of U.S$145 per barrel, and later in 2008/9 oil prices dropped below $40 per barrel, not only petroleum oil prices but prices every other industrial commodities fell and fell sharply lower as there was total carnage in commodity markets across the world as a consequence of 2008 global financial crisis, all base metals prices declined or rather collapse due to 2008 financial meltdown, banking financial troubles of 2008/9 plunged the global economy into deep recession, the financial crisis played significant role in failure of key businesses and declines in consumer wealth was estimated in trillions of U.S dollars, The active phase of the crisis, which manifested as a **liquidity crisis,** can be dated from August 9, 2007, when **BNP Paribas** terminated withdrawals from three hedge funds citing "a complete evaporation of liquidity. Sometime towards the end of 2008 the U.S Central Bank "Federal Reserve" taking bold initiatives but also perhaps most "convenient one" to halt deteriorating health of world's economy and U.S's in particular announced economic stimulus package QE (quantitative easing) and started printing fresh money in trillions of dollars, in subsequent months and years other countries as well started announcing their own QE programmes Japan, China and European central bank they all did what U.S did that was printing cash money, massive cash liquidity injected into the banking system and ultra-cheap credit made available to the businesses to borrow helped in reviving economic growth and trend reversal was led by stupendous China economic growth, due to heavy demand for industrial commodities and minerals and petroleum oil and gas from India and China the commodity markets started to recover back again in 2010, between 2011/13 the prices of almost all commodities rallied remarkably, Base-metals, precious metals, and more importantly the prices of petroleum crude oil & gas moved sharply higher.

The sharp increase in prices of various commodities between 2011 and 2013, tempted and encouraged the mineral mining companies to extract more minerals from beneath the surface of earth, and oil exploration companies drilled more oil wells to pump out more oil and gas, the manufacturing industries in China kept producing more industrial goods and consumer products, but what goes up has to come down, China's economic growth considerably slowed down beginning of 2014, due to demand recession for consumer products, and over production and excessive supply of minerals and petroleum oil and gas, created glut in the international markets, incredibly high production of durables and consumer products on assumption that demand for consumer items will only keep growing, but contrary to high expectation there was a subsequent sharp decline in demand for durable goods which caused a monumental fall in prices of commodities in 2015, massive drop in China's stock-markets in June –July of year 2015, demand for luxury items and for other consumer product further declined because the Chinese purchasing power reduced considerably, sharp fall in commodity prices that began in middle of 2014 and continued to fall and remained at lower level throughout year 2015 literally ruined the economies of resource dependant countries, turbulent in commodity markets caused uncertainty in Forex currency markets, Russia, Venezuela, Saudi Arabia, Iraq and Brazil etc all such major commodity producing and exporting countries suffered immense pain and economic hardship, due to decline in prices of commodities they produce and sharp fall in value of their respective country's currency, substantially reduced and eroded the purchasing power of resource dependant countries governments and of their citizens, when domestic economy is greatly affected by commodity price shifts, then that country's currency exchange rate is especially vulnerable, but not just commodity producing nations suffered economic troubles, also other countries as well suffered extreme hardship and uncertainty in forex and commodity markets considerably slowed down their economic growth.

Digging tunnels into the earth's crust, to extract minerals buried underground, digging and drilling deeper and deeper holes to extract minerals from the ground, to make and earn more money quickly and easily without any concern or remorse as to how much excessive mining and exploration will or could harm environment and cause climatic problems. Due to QE (quantitative easing) and frequent economic stimulus packages of rich industrialized countries in the aftermath of 2008/9 financial crisis to spur global economic growth, easy cash liquidity made available in the banking system had enticed and encouraged companies in the business of mining and oil & gas exploration to produce more output, due to massive increase in production of crude oil and other minerals like Iron-ore, copper and bauxite etc," supply exceeds demand, so slowing global economic growth which apparently reduced demand for various industrial commodities, hence due to huge oversupply of various commodities and large pile up of unsold inventories mainly of finish durable goods, so combination of factors like large pile of input materials both raw materials as well as of finish items and products in some of the prominent industrialized nations, so reduced demand caused monumental decline in prices of commodities in international commodity markets in 2015.

Uncertain situation became even more uncertain, the beginning of year 2016 proved to be nightmarish not only for the commodity producing and exporting countries but for the entire world's financial markets, in January-2016 prices of petroleum crude oil suffered bigger loses when prices declined below U.S$30 per barrel, Investors were jittery because of uncertainty in commodity markets which apparently created problems in Forex markets besides uncertainty with regards to future of principle resource dependant and commodity producing countries, nervous investors started unloading their investments apart from mining and oil exploration companies banking and financial companies share values fell sharply on major bourses across the globe.

Mounting concerns and worries about rising fiscal budget deficits of large commodity producing and exporting countries, hence assessing the ground realities for the first time ever perhaps in Jan-2016 trade analysts and economists started predicting that two of world's biggest oil and gas producing countries **Saudi Arabia** and **Russia,** there were/are apprehension amongst economists that if crude oil and gas prices remains subdued and keeps trading in lower range for longer period of time than these two prominent oil producing and exporting countries will be financially bankrupt, not just the Saudis and Russians but many other principle commodity producing countries would suffer extreme economic and social pain if corrective steps not taken and quick solutions not found. When there is a problem obviously we need to find a solution, now with regards to these beleaguered resource dependent nations economic problems which needs amicable solution, so now, if to fix economic problems if same measures is used that is of Printing money, create more cash liquidity to create bigger demand for consumer products, well I'm afraid printing more money to create more demand for durables and consumer goods may perhaps give a short term respite, but over longer term will only harm humanity and increase global warming and cause more climatic problems.

Monumental decline in commodity prices in 2015/16 had nasty economic and social consequences and had devastating negative impact on global economic growth and destroyed livelihoods of millions of people, Hundreds of billions of U.S Dollars that were earlier earmarked for massive expansion and or for new business investments in mining minerals and oil and gas exploration projects had to be either suspended for indefinite period of time or cancelled all together, also many existing companies in business of oil & gas exploration and mineral mining because of sustain lower profitability and losses suffered had to adopt drastic measures and were compelled to reduce workforce, hundreds of thousands of people lost their jobs, the magnitude and negative effects of **Commodity Crisis** in 2014/15 which precipitated problems in Forex (foreign exchange currency) and

Capital markets were more severe and brutal than compare to 2008/9 financial crisis.

An asset bubble can be also aggravated by a supply shortage, if investors think there isn't enough of the stuff to go around. Asset bubbles are often initially caused by **low interest rates**. Low rates create an over-expansion of the >**money supply**. Investors can borrow cheaply, but can't receive much return on bonds, so they look for another **asset class**. A speculative bubble is usually caused by exaggerated expectations of future growth, price appreciation, or other events that could cause an increase in asset values. This drives trading volumes higher, and as more investors **rally** around the heightened expectation, buyers outnumber sellers, pushing prices beyond what an objective analysis of intrinsic value would suggest. Prices rise quickly over a short period of time, and are not supported by underlying demand for the product itself. It's a bubble when investors bid up the price beyond any real sustainable value. This price spikes often occur when investors all flock to a particular asset class, such as the stock market, real estate or commodities. The bubble is not completed until prices fall back down to normalized levels; this usually involves a period of steep decline in price during which most investors panic and sell out of their investments.

Economic bubble in **Japan** from 1986 to 1991 in which **real estate** and **stock market** prices were greatly inflated. The bubble was characterized by rapid acceleration of asset prices and overheated economic activity, as well as an uncontrolled money supply and credit expansion. More specifically, over-confidence and speculation regarding asset and stock prices had been closely associated with excessive monetary easing policy at the time. By August 1990, the **Nikkei stock index** had plummeted to half its peak by the time of the fifth monetary tightening by the **Bank of Japan.** By late 1991, the asset price began to fall. This decline resulted in a huge accumulation of **non-performing assets loans** (NPL), causing difficulties for many financial institutions. The bursting of the Japanese asset price bubble contributed to what many call the **Lost Decade**.

There is no doubt that a global climate regime on the basis of international cooperation is needed to prevent some of the disastrous consequences of climate change. Its challenge is that it must include the commitment of developed countries such as the U.S. and the EU (European Union) as well as the commitment of large developing countries that have fast growing economies and a rapid increase in emissions such as China and India. This is difficult because it raises questions of global climate justice, historic liability and equal rights, i.e. whether developing countries should enjoy the same right to economic growth based on fossil fuels as the industrialized countries have experienced over the past century. Even if environmental costs were distributed equally to every person on earth, developing countries would still bear 80% of the burden (because they account for 80% of world population). As it is, they bear an even greater share, though their citizens' carbon footprints are much smaller. To solve critical Economic and social problems one needs to apply their mind, you need to have high quality **analytical skills** and more importantly need to have **critical thinking skills** so that your mind can think of creative ideas to solve critical and complex problems.

That's exactly what is not happening, the Central banks governors, the economic advisors and policies planners, the thinkers and decision makers and decision takers around the world it seems have seriously ran out of ideas. To ensure sustain economic growth and to improve standard of living of citizens of your country, the government officials, bureaucrats and politicians need to step out of their staggeringly decorated offices and needs to work on ground level, it is only through hard work that we can get sustain and equal economic growth and business development, such **short-cut measures** when politicians and government officials think that we'll keep printing unlimited amount of money as long as it is needed and everything will take care of itself and every other things will automatically get sorted out, in 21st the economists and policy planners of leading industrialized countries and Multilateral Development Banks feels that no need for us to step out of our office, just order Printing more money and all will be fine.

No dear, **Quantitative Easing** only help fuels rally and boom in stock-markets and property markets and share value of few prominent companies rises higher and higher thereby helps increase wealth and net-worth of few influential people, rich becomes richer and a person who is millionaire becomes billionaire, and that's why each time stock-markets fall 8 or 10%, one of the leading industrialized country high ranking central bank officer will come forward and assures the market players that their central bank is ready to do more, which obviously means ready to print more currency notes, frequent economic stimulus packages only helps few voracious and egocentric individuals and affluent families make oodles of money, for the rest of the world's population it is only hard work provided they manage to find job for themselves or else its only misery.

But, how do we earn money? Is it possible for every living human in this world to have sufficient money to meet all his/her basic needs and requirements so as to live life with comfort and dignity?

One Fat medical bill or one failed crop (agriculture crop) can severely impact the living standard and lowers social status of the affected family, reduces status from upper middleclass to lower middleclass.

Yes, it is true that medical science and technology have made remarkable progress, our intelligent Scientists and Engineers have developed advanced scientific technology, all kinds of brutal ailments and diseases can be treated and be cured, but very few people in the world can afford or have access to best medical-care facilities and medical treatments, otherwise, for the large population of the world when they experience any kind of serious health problems like for example "fatal injuries, cancer, diabetes or cardio problems," for an average person around the world it is so difficult to have or to afford best quality medical treatment because it is so damn expensive, according to some estimates it has been found that staggering 75% of the world's population is medically vulnerable and can't afford to pay steep medical bills it is beyond their reach and means.

Citizens of rich developed countries do enjoy some privileges, government healthcare and services departments of developed countries do provide best possible basic medical healthcare facilities to their citizens, also medi-care insurance policy is available to be purchased at affordable price, but for the rest of the countries in the world and large population living in developing and 3rd world countries things are extremely difficult, people living in poor undeveloped nations for example Indian sub-continent countries and in African countries large percentage of population are so desperately poor that they can't even afford to buy simple basic medicines like Cough syrup, nose drops, or eye drops.

Affordability or unaffordability is one of the factor, whether or not if a person living in an underdeveloped country can afford to buy medicines and afford best possible medical treatment, as it is said that "health is wealth," what we need in the country where we live in must have efficient and well organized medical system and well entrenched healthcare facilities, but there apparently in another bigger perspective, for inadequate and appalling healthcare facilities and service in many of the underdeveloped and 3rd world countries, and that is because of widespread corruption and mismanagement of public healthcare system.

Most of the medical practitioners and medical staff and professionals in developing and 3rd world countries or for that matter perhaps even in developed countries have inadequate, insufficient and incomprehensible knowledge about medical terminology, medical diagnosis of patient and understanding of medicines, and most of the medical professionals and doctors often goof up majorly in diagnosing their patients and often make erroneous assumption and renders inappropriate medical treatment and prescribes incorrect medicines. Here have a listen to this, there is a joke on the street in Indian cities that "India's Medical and Public healthcare system is more corrupt than compare to India's political system," yes, Indian sub-continent countries which also includes countries like Pakistan and Bangladesh there is high level of corruption in medical and healthcare system, the healthcare facilities and medical services in Indian sub-continent countries is thoroughly disorganised and inefficient. Do some reality check and you'll discover the true reason as to why in so many countries the Public healthcare facilities are so appalling, and the most likely reason is that in India, Pakistan or in African countries like Nigeria and in several south-American countries large percentage of practicing doctors and other medical professionals have allegedly obtained medical degrees and certificates by fraudulent means.

In India for example it is allege that a person who wish to become "Doctor, lawyer or engineer" and if he/she is able to or willing to spend 2 or 3 million Rupees, so a person who is willing to spend money can conveniently obtain higher educational and diploma certificates and degrees, so be it India, Pakistan, China or Nigeria the education system itself is devastatingly corrupt, any person who has money and influence can easily manipulate the system and can win favours for himself/herself and obtain top tier jobs.

Corrective steps and preventive measures needs to be taken to weed out corruption from Education system, but corruption in Education is not restricted to any one particular country, it's largely a worldwide phenomenon, Pakistan and Nigeria as well are notorious for trading Fake educational degrees, certificates and forged documents, there is more corruption in some countries and less in some countries but there is corruption in high places which is an undeniable truth, corruption in Education systems destroys life of younger generation.

Article title "**The Economic and Social Implications of Epidemics**" explains; "Throughout history emerging infectious diseases have shaped the course of human history and have caused incalculable misery and death. New advances in science, technology and medicine have helped us gain ground against certain infectious diseases. However, even in the twenty-first century infectious diseases continue to emerge at a rapid pace. Many Emerging Infectious Diseases (EIDs) have been catalyzed by wars, loss of social cohesion, and natural disasters. Under these conditions and in addition to microbial or viral virulence factors, a contagious disease may lead to an epidemic outbreak. An epidemic is categorized as a fast growing outbreak that affects many people almost instantly, usually within a city. If the epidemic is not sufficiently contained it can become a pandemic outbreak, that has no social or geographical boundaries.

EIDs pose a major risk to the health and welfare of global human and animal populations. The staggering impact on a population can be both directly and indirectly. Human populations are directly at risk from infection and indirectly at risk through the impact on their food supply. The risks associated with food supply include the economic losses related to the culling of animals and the unavailability of food caused by real or suspected contamination. In addition epidemics have the potential to severely disrupt global supply chains and further harm human health. An epidemic's impact on the economy can vary based on its imminent and long-term severity. This is influenced by the rate of hospitalizations, insurance premiums, outpatient visits and the largest contributor, death. Most economic models agree that death causes the greatest economic decline with a yearly cost of billions on the economy."...........

The economic costs of epidemics are often out of proportion to their death toll. The outbreak of Severe Acute Respiratory Syndrome (SARS) in 2003 is estimated to have caused over $50 billion-worth of damage to the global economy, despite infecting only about 8,000 people and causing fewer than 800 deaths. That is because panic and confusion can be as disruptive as the disease itself. Studies of past outbreaks have shown that lethal diseases that lack a cure tend to provoke overreactions. This is true even if the risk of transmission is low, as is the case with Ebola.

Governments walk a fine line between limiting the spread of a disease and causing needless disruption. Panic is avoided not just by combating an epidemic, but by being seen to do so. Transparency is important. By disclosing the extent of an outbreak, governments limit the spread of rumours and encourage an appropriate response from business and the public. But there is also the risk that weak governments will simply expose their impotence.

Scientific and technological advances, such as genomics and informatics, extend the limits of knowledge and human potential more rapidly than their implications can be absorbed and acted upon. At the same time, people, products, and germs migrate and the world's demographics are shifting in ways that challenge public and private resources. The systems and entities that protect and promote the public's health, already challenged by problems like obesity, toxic environments, a large uninsured population, and health disparities, must also confront emerging threats, such as antimicrobial resistance and bioterrorism. The social, cultural, and global contexts of the people's health are also undergoing rapid and dramatic change. Health is a primary public good because many aspects of human potential such as employment, social relationships, and political participation are contingent on it. In view of the value of health to employers, business, communities, and society in general, creating the conditions for people to be healthy should also be a shared social goal.

These days, development teams are asked to do more with less because companies are reluctant to staff up in these uncertain economic times. Right, wrong or indifferent, if you are asked to be a lean team (i.e. no new resources in the foreseeable future), then you need to operate as a lean team and recognize that doing "less is more."

In a widespread public healthcare emergency, there will be more people who need healthcare than there are resources available to help them. Making decisions about how to use these limited resources will be difficult. Hospital personnel and public health officials need to know how to make decisions in these difficult moments in a way that reflects the values of the communities in which those decisions will be made.

Human history is undoubtedly stained with the blood of men, women and children killed in war, but it is disease that is the world's biggest killer - and it does not discriminate between race, creed or colour.

If healthcare is a problem, there are many other challenges to deal with in 21st century, one of the most pressing problem is hunger and poverty, according to some surveys and research studies have found Worldwide there are 1.5 billion people who can't afford to eat healthy nutritional food because they have little or no money, but there also is another reason behind hunger and starvation, that is brazen wastage of food, roughly one third of food produce in the world for human consummation each year --- approximately 1.3 billion tonnes – gets lost or wasted.

A report prepared by **"United Nation Environment Programme' Food Waste: The Facts,"** has written; "When we scrape off our dishes after a large meal, too full to finish the remaining scraps on our plate, we rarely pause and think about the significance of our action. It seems routine to us: if we have leftover food scraps that are unfit for eating, shouldn't they be thrown in the garbage? Our routine practices, unfortunately, make it difficult for us to conceptualize the magnitude of global food waste. The problem is bigger than we think.

According to a recent report by UNEP and the World Resources Institute (WRI), about one-third of all food produced worldwide, worth around US$1 trillion, gets lost or wasted in food production and consumption systems. When this figure is converted to calories, this means that about 1 in 4 calories intended for consumption is never actually eaten. In a world full of hunger, volatile food prices, and social unrest, these statistics are more than just shocking: they are environmentally, morally and economically outrageous.
Let's start with some basic statistics about food waste in North America and around the world.

Worldwide Food Waste Facts

- Every year, consumers in industrialized countries waste almost as much food as the entire net food production of sub-Saharan Africa (222 million vs. 230 million tons)
- The amount of food lost and wasted every year is equal to more than half of the world's annual cereals crops (2.3 billion tons in 2009/10)

North American Food Waste Facts
- In the USA, organic waste is the second highest component of landfills, which are the largest source of methane emissions
- In the USA, 30-40% of the food supply is wasted, equalling more than 20 pounds of food per person per month.".................

The impact of food waste is not just financial. Environmentally, food waste leads to wasteful use of chemicals such as fertilizers and pesticides; more fuel used for transportation; and more rotting food, creating more methane – one of the most harmful greenhouse gases that contributes to climate change. Methane is 23 times more potent than CO_2 as a greenhouse gas. The vast amount of food going to landfills makes a significant contribution to global warming.

Food loss and waste also amount to a major squandering of resources, including water, land, energy, labour and capital and needlessly produce greenhouse gas emissions, contributing to global warming and climate change.

In developing countries food waste and losses occur mainly at early stages of the food value chain and can be traced back to financial, managerial and technical constraints in harvesting techniques as well as storage –and cooling facilities. Thus, a strengthening of the supply chain through the support farmers and investments in infrastructure, transportation, as well as in an expansion of the food –and packaging industry could help to reduce the amount of food loss and waste.

In medium- and high-income countries food is wasted and lost mainly at later stages in the supply chain. Differing from the situation in developing countries, the behaviour of consumers plays a huge part in industrialized countries. Moreover, the study identified a lacking coordination between actors in the supply chain as a contributing factor. Farmer-buyer agreements can be helpful to increase the level of coordination. Additionally, raising awareness among industries, retailers and consumers as well as finding beneficial use for save food that is presently thrown away are useful measures to decrease the amount of losses and waste.

While hunger and poverty is problematic, overeating and obesity is another bigger trillion dollar problem, Article title **"Obesity Costs Global Economy \$2 Trillion" has stated in – CNN Money;** "The obesity epidemic has grown too big to ignore.

A new report by McKinsey estimates that obesity is costing the global economy \$2 trillion per year. That makes it nearly as damaging as armed conflict or smoking, according to the consultants.

More than 2 billion people -- or almost 30% of the global population -- are currently considered overweight or obese, and the problem is expected to get worse.

Based on current trends, nearly half of the world's adults will be overweight or obese by 2030.

"Obesity, which should be preventable, is now responsible for about 5% of all deaths worldwide," the report stated.

Smoking is considered the most expensive man-made burden on the economy with a cost of \$2.1 trillion, followed closely by armed conflict.

Related: Employers are measuring workers' waistlines

The damage caused by obesity mainly comes from lost productivity due to disability and premature death, and higher healthcare costs.

So what should be done?

Among the options, governments can redesign cities to encourage cycling or subsidize healthy meals in schools. Both would generate a good return on their investment.

But the **fast food giants** need to play ball too, by changing the menus in their restaurants. That's much easier said than done.

Burger King (BKW) said in August that it was removing its **lower-calorie fries** from most of its restaurants because the product had proved less popular than it hoped.

Burger King billed the Satisfries as having 40% less fat and 30% fewer calories than McDonald's fries."…………

A report by **McKinsey & Company**, which studied 44 different ways of combating obesity, found the global impact is the equivalent to smoking or armed violence, war and terrorism.
In the UK the burden on the economy is £47 billion a year - greater than the impact of armed violence, war and terrorism - while in the U.S. it is £663 billion.
The researchers have called on global governments, healthcare systems, retailers and food and drinks manufacturers to 'coordinate' their response to tackle the crisis head on.

We are now in the middle of a global economic and political crisis, the intensity of which is unprecedented in the post–World War II era. The strains from this crisis, which takes different forms in different countries, have spread throughout the world. Many governments have already fallen, and more will do so in the years ahead because of persistent unemployment and popular anger and distrust. In 2011 in China there were 189,000 riots and mass incidents due to local grievances and broader issues. Unemployment, inflation, and painful budgetary dilemmas have made the management of politics extremely difficult for leaders all over the world. And we are now only at the middle, not the end, of this painful protracted period of economic distress and popular discontent.

In the 14th century, **Moroccan** traveler and scholar **Ibn Battuta** made a long journey to Africa and Asia. He reached China in April 1345 after a stay in India before serving as an envoy of **Sultan Muhammad Tughlaq** of the Indian **Tughlaq dynasty** to China. He wrote "China is the safest, best regulated of countries for a traveler. A man may go by himself on a nine-month journey, carrying with him a large sum of money, without any fear. Silk is used for clothing even by poor monks and beggars. Its porcelains are the finest of all makes of pottery and its hens are bigger than geese in our country.".

While rest of the world enviably looks at China's economic growth prospect, and large Multinational companies and bankers are keen to invest their money in china hoping to earn higher returns on invested capital, but it seems the China's nationals at least some of the Chinese are it seems less optimistic about China's long term economic growth prospect or may be some wealthy Chinese feels less secure to have their money invested in domestic Chinese companies, business and properties or their money deposited in China's commercial banks, that seems to be the most likely reason because between 2010 and 2015 thousands of super rich and wealthy Chinese have taken their money out of China and it has been reported that they've invested substantial amount of money overseas, money earned by fair means or allegedly by unfair and corrupt means, most conservative estimates suggest that the rich Chinese have invested well over U.S.$200 Billion buying assets and properties in countries like Australia, U.S.A, U.K and few other prominent countries, walk on the streets of any American or Australian cities and you will see many Chinese owned businesses, properties and homes.

When declining trend first began to emerge and there were imminent signs of slowdown in China's manufacturing sector in the beginning of 2013, to prevent downslide the government authorities and China's Central bank did what other developed countries Central bankers do, they as well started lowering interest rates and injected massive amount of fresh Cash liquidity into their banking system for obvious purpose that was for common people and for the businesses and industries to borrow more money, when returns on fixed income debt paper and bank deposits are low and unattractive, especially the middle-income and lower middle income individual people and families finds another alternate investments avenue and where else will they invest their money but in stock markets, it is alleged that the Chinese government authorities had subtly encouraged the lower middle income Chinese folks to invest their money in China's stock markets, when large number of people started investing money in China's stock markets there was a spectacular spurt in 2014/15 witnessed in the China stock-markets, valuations of listed Chinese companies extraordinarily kept rising, but then came the inevitable crash, in June and July of 2015 China's stock market fell nearly 50% from its peak, as it always happens many of those unfortunate lower middle income folks lost their money and lost it heavily, so the steep losses that millions of Chinese suffered due to stock market crash it caused further harm to China's economic growth. What is or what was required to do initially when there were visible sign of imminent economic slowdown, it was for the China's Central bank "**People's Bank of China**" to have aggressively **devalued** its currency **Yuan** against other major international currencies, China's Central Bank by strongly devaluing its currency would have also succeeded in restricting the outflow of money from China, a move that would have prevented rich and alleged corrupt Chinese from taking money out of their country, and also would have added much needed strength to its tiring manufacturing sector and perhaps would have saved many job losses.

There is this misconception in minds of many or to say it is a myth that lower commodity prices benefits companies and helps spur economic growth of principle commodity importing countries, now like China's economy registered considerable slowdown in 2014/15, similarly China's neighboring country India's economic growth has also been tepid or even worse than that of China. This is a false perception created by many that massive fall in commodity prices significantly helps growth of commodity importing countries, India is principle importer of many commodities, particularly India imports substantial quantity of petroleum crude oil and gas, despite 65% fall or slide in prices of crude oil, yet India's economy between July-2014 and December-2015 has remained lukewarm, but Indian government agencies according to some vague mathematical calculation published figures which quoted 7% plus annual economic growth, however we need to do some real reality check to discover the fact of as to how India's economy has performed during the period between July-2014 and December-2015, since July-2014 when internationally commodity prices started to decline and remained at lower level for the whole of calendar year 2015, during this period as per available information, Indian companies financial performance remained stubbornly below par, overall Indian corporates reported poor sales growth and profitability (bottom line) of most Indian companies remained weak, India's export fell between 24 to 28%, Indian Rupee in value fell against major international currencies, Indian Rupee against U.S Dollar fell 12%, India is world's 2nd most populous nation, hence it requires to create millions of job each year, but during this period as per figures published by government agencies only 525,000 new jobs were created not to ignore the fact that many businesses were shut during this period hence there were potential job losses, so there was appalling job growth rate in India, but more severe pain for Indian citizen was/is the exponential increase in prices of Food, prices of fruits, vegetables and medicines became unfordable for average Indian citizen and not to forget the fact that India has highest number of people living in poverty in the world. Adding more problems to Indian economy was sharp increase in Banks "Non-Performing asset loans (Bad loans/Debt)," more pain in form of rising unemployment and growing poverty, as 60% of India's population lives in rural India in villages hence rural population is overwhelmingly dependent on agriculture, and agriculture sector in India is worst hit, agro industry and farmers are considered backbone of India's economy but between 2014/15 thousands of debt-ridden and poverty stricken **farmers** in despair and agony committed suicides. So brutal fall of Chinese stock markets both Chinese and

Indians trimming their expenditure because of subdued economic performance of China and India, this facts loudly and clearly indicates us that steep decline in commodity prices only exacerbate situation and further weakens economic fundamentals and does not augur to well at ground level.

With regards to India's great economic growth story, there was lot of hype and hoopla, between 2014/15, so much hype created in media, as if India has become economic superpower of the world, it was all creation of Rightist control media, even the western media fell prey, the western media without doing any ground work and never really bothered to have a ground level perspective and to do thorough reality check of ground reality in India to verify the facts, the western media as well over reported, overstated and over hyped India's economic growth story. India has as of 2015 population of over 1.25 Billion people, maybe few tens of million people in India are affluent and financially secured and have great spending power, but for remaining hundreds of millions of Indian citizens for them their day to day life is extremely difficult and distressful and devastatingly challenging to say the least.

The job of the government in each country has to be that of an regulator and monitor, and not of or be seen as manipulator, Capital & Financial Markets needs to be well regulated and the functioning should be transparent, administration and management needs to be made accountable, as long as market players are following the rules, government officers and ministers should not be concern and not lose their sleep over whether the listed companies share value (prices) are falling sharply lower or rising higher.

To understand more; touching base with another perspective "**Bad news is not Bad; yes, in fact, Bad news is considered Good news**," it so happens that be it the U.S.A, Germany, China, Japan or any other or many more countries which have *Capitalist economic system*, whenever their respective country's **economic ministry or economic statistic department** publishes dismal economic data suggesting weaker economic growth, figures indicating lower GDP growth rate, rise in unemployment, drop in monthly retail sales, so whenever such dismal economic data are made public, a significantly prominent section of society, the Stock-markets traders and investors rejoice that moment and expectation runs high because investing community firmly believes that weaker economic growth will compel and force country's politicians and central bank to act decisively by taking more bold steps and measures to stimulate their country's economic growth, and obviously for that purpose the central bank chief will have to announce more liberal market friendly **monetary and credit policy**, and will inject higher amount of cash-liquidity into the financial system to stimulate economic growth, boosting public spending to increase consumption. The monetary and credit policies are well coordinated among central bankers of leading industrialized countries.

If printing money is not enough than as another measures to create cash liquidity in the system is to adopt **negative interest rate policy**, wherein the depositors do not earn interest for depositing money instead they have to pay charges or to say penalty to park their surplus cash with central banks or maybe even with regular commercial banks. As of 2016 few exemplary examples are **Bank of Japan** and **European Central Bank** are among few of those leading industrialized nations central banks which have adopted negative interest rate policy.

Central banks use their deposit to influence how banks handle their reserves. In the case of negative rates, central banks want to dissuade lenders (commercial banks) from parking cash with them. The hope is that they will use that money to lend to individuals and businesses, which in turn will spend the money and boost the economy and contribute to inflation.

It is also aiming to force investors to shift money out of bank accounts and into higher-yielding assets.

Since central banks provide a **benchmark** for all borrowing costs, negative rates spread to a **range of fixed-income securities**. By the end of 2015, about *a third* of the debt issued by euro zone governments had negative yields. That means investors holding to maturity won't get all their money back. Banks have been **reluctant** to pass on negative rates for fear of losing customers.

A negative interest rate means the **central bank** and perhaps private banks will charge negative interest: instead of receiving money on deposits, depositors must pay regularly to keep their money with the bank. This is intended to incentivize banks to lend money more freely and businesses and individuals to invest, lend, and spend money rather than pay a fee to keep it safe.

"Don't keep the **Powder dry**;" central banks actually coercing commercial lending banks and financial institutions to lend money to industries and businesses and also to individual people without any rational thinking and without dwelling much about borrower's repayment capacity, also exerting psychological pressure on individual people that for higher returns invest their savings and money in high-yielding assets, but for higher returns on capital to invest money in stock-markets or in precious metals (gold, platinum etc), or in high-yielding junk bonds or if in property, such investments are not without risk but full of risk and higher degree of uncertainty.

Wealthy families and business lobbyists mounts pressure on politicians and politicians and bureaucrats in turn puts pressure on central bank chief to take pragmatic steps and announce market friendly Credit and Monetary policy, with sly motive to create asset inflation, to ensure boom in stock-markets, so the mantra is borrow more spend more, but does anyone bothers or is ever concern about that those businesses and individual people who'll borrow money also have to repay money.

When inexpensive loans and abundant cash credit is easily made available, when borrowing cost are lowered to record low levels, nature of people as well of business owners in general is to take advantage of prevailing situation, so when money is available easily and cheaply they get excited and tempted to borrow more and more money and frivolously overspend money on buying unwanted items. People in general and business owners in particular overindulging in speculating and gambling or starting non-sustainable and unproductive business ventures, over producing industrial goods and consumer products, and one day the inevitable happens when they have exceeded their spending limits and exhausted their purchasing power, they are unable to repay the money back to their creditors, that's the time when many lending institutions and Banks will have long list of large scale loan defaulters, and all these combination of reasons and factors and also when businesses fails obviously many people lose their jobs so than due to massive job losses it creates a brutal long lasting economic recession and which in turn causes too many social problems and troubles in society. Not only economic recession, but we also have to keep in mind that excessive mining of minerals and exploration of petroleum oil and gas, as minerals and crude oil is/are crucial raw material to manufacture all kinds and types of industrial and consumer products, so excessive mining to extract more minerals profoundly and severely harms environment and ruins earth's atmosphere, deteriorating weather condition is danger for each of us as it risk survival of humanity on this planet.

Humans are "eating away at our own life support systems" at a rate unseen in the past 10,000 years by degrading land and freshwater systems, emitting greenhouse gases and releasing vast amounts of agricultural chemicals into the environment, Most underground mining operations increase sedimentation in nearby rivers through their use of hydraulic pumps and suction dredges; blasting with hydraulic pumps removes ecologically valuable topsoil containing seed banks, making it difficult for vegetation to recover. Underground mining has the potential for tunnel collapses and land subsidence. It involves large-scale movements of waste rock and vegetation, similar to open pit mining. Additionally, like most traditional forms of mining, underground mining can release toxic compounds into the air and water. As water takes on harmful concentrations of minerals and heavy metals, it becomes a contaminant. Deforestation due to mining leads to the disintegration of biomes and contributes to the effects of erosion. Thus, a large-scale mining process can affect the environment, including the human environment miles away from the original mining site. Exposure to chemicals poisons the human body causing everything from skin rashes to cancer. Drinking water with lead and other chemicals can affect babies and cause birth defects.

In modern times most Central Banks adopting more liberal and easy **monetary policy** and easy Credit policy has have had brutal and killing impact on **Fixed income markets,** Fixed income which gives assured annual returns and considered highly safe, for hundreds of years in the past ages common people and investors used to invest their hard earn money and savings in Fixed income securities like Fixed deposit in Bank or Post-office, or they use to invest in government debt instruments and bonds, and use to earn decent assured annual income, in more recent times now in 21st century with banks having reduced interest rates to near Zero%, and government securities of many rich industrialized countries giving dismal 2% or 3% annual returns, even in many developing countries where interest-rate on bank fixed deposit or government bonds are in lower single digit, in times of distressfully lower banking interest-rates, many people are left with no other choice but to take risk of either investing their hard earn money in stock-markets or in **"triple B or C"** rated companies **junk bonds,** such investments which are high-risk and sometimes highly rewarding, and then there are also lunatics who invest their money in **Ponzi schemes** and end up losing their shirt.

I must say, that, 21st century politicians are ruthless because they are simply forcing humble people to take higher and higher unwise risk.

When so ever a country or the global economy is plunged into recession or when businesses are experiencing slowdown, so the best way and a good strategy of dealing with uncertain business environment is to allow the recession to run its course, as there is a saying "don't try catching a falling knife," don't try any desperate measures and take ill-timed decisions to contain recession, any massive fall or sharp downward price correction in stock-markets, should be welcomed because when share value of prominent companies are down and available at distinctly lower rates, it provides another large section of society an option or an opportunity to buy and to make investments in blue chip companies shares which are available at lower valuation. Therefore economic recession is not always a bad thing to happen, at times recession opens up windows of opportunities for large section of society and gives another chance or an opportunity for wide section of society to take calculated risk and to succeed in life by investing their time and money in promising business ventures.

Here I would like to emphatically and categorically like to say, that NOT the Islamic Terrorism or terrorists that we humans need to fear most, but, it is the Central Bank chiefs, those people responsible for printing unprecedented amount of cash money, to artificially spur their own country's as well to boost global economic growth, are actually the biggest enemy of humanity, it is they (central bankers) who will be responsible for destroying humanity and not the Islamic terrorists as many of you folks fear and wholeheartedly believe they will.

Article title "**The Politics and the Economics of the Global Financial Crisis,**" "First, let me make a general point about political instability. Two-thousand five-hundred years ago, Plato in his Republic and Dialogues, gave us an intellectual framework for what can happen to forms of government over time. Plato writes that democracy is not a permanent condition, but only a stage in a broader political cycle that begins with tyranny, evolves into oligarchy, shifts into democracy, falls into anarchy, and then returns again to tyranny.

Plato describes this process. He writes that when tyrants like Mao and Stalin pass away, a collective leadership process, which he calls an oligarchy, often replaces it. Initially the people welcome the new oligarchy because it is such an improvement over the bloody tyrant, and people often view the new oligarchs as patriotic servants of the country. Over time, however, Plato writes that the oligarchs become corrupted and lose their prestige, which appears to be happening today in China and elsewhere. Pressures then build to broaden the base of the oligarchy until a democracy evolves. This democracy, Plato asserts, can eventually fall into anarchy after politicians promise election benefits to the people that exceed the ability of the state to afford. Plato says that eventually the drones in the hive outnumber the worker bees, and the hive itself becomes unsustainable. Shortages, inflation, and various destabilizing social phenomena appear, as happened in the final days of the Yeltsin period in Russia. This produces popular anger and eventually a brief period of anarchy. Anarchy never lasts very long, however, and often a new tyrant emerges from this anarchy, who brutally establishes his vision of order. The challenge Plato's thesis offers us today is to preserve our precious democracies by managing our current economic problems intelligently and not letting them deteriorate to the point that demagogues from the political world are given space to return to power, as happened in the 1930s.

But as we think about Plato's political cycles, it is important to remember that history suggests that such cycles tend to run clockwise, not counterclockwise. In other words, democracies usually emerge from decayed authoritarian regimes. They seldom evolve from angry, confused, and violent mobs in the streets. A new tyrant is far more likely to emerge from such conditions. We are all hoping that the Arab Spring will prove to be an exception to this pattern.

So this Platonic cycle is the larger political framework that I would like to ask you to bear in mind as we move forward to address the very difficult, painful, and multifaceted global economic crisis we now face.".......

Debt levels across the Eurozone continue to rocket, with the monetary bloc's debt reaching nearly 92% in 2014 - the **highest level since the single currency was introduced** in 1999.

Increases in debt across the continent show that countries are struggling to take control of their public expenditure, while the countries with the smallest total debt are often those that have seen the largest increases over recent years.
Just three European countries have managed to reduce their total debt between the first quarter of 2012 and the last quarter of 2014, while eight have managed to do so as a proportion of their GDP.
Norway has reduced its total debt by 17.9% over the three year period, and by 11.4% when measuring it as a proportion of GDP.
Total public debt increased by its fastest rate in Estonia, which has seen an 87 per cent increase - from €1.1bn in 2012 to €2.1bn in 2014. Bulgaria and Slovenia have also seen increases of over three quarters in three years.

Article tile **"Risks of Rising Consumer Debt – Money Zine"** writes; "Over the past decade, we've seen lower interest rates, a broken housing market, and virtually unlimited options when it comes to personal loans. The end result is that Americans are borrowing money at a record pace; consumer debt is on the rise.

In order to know whether or not rising debt is a problem in America, it's important to understand some basic economic rules. For example, when a consumer buys something, the money spent doesn't simply stop at that store.

In fact, experts believe that around 70% of the U.S. gross domestic product (a common measure of economic growth) is derived from consumer spending. This means even relatively small changes in spending habits can have fairly large effects on the health of the economy. Perhaps the best way to understand debt's effect on the economy is explained through an example.

Let's say a consumer decides they want to buy a new car or truck. To buy the truck, the consumer is going to increase their debt load. They're going to borrow money.

When the purchase is finalized, the money doesn't stop there; some of it keeps flowing. The salesperson collects a commission, and the dealership buys another car from the factory. The salesperson now has some extra money to spend. The factory pays its workers to produce more trucks. They purchase parts from their suppliers, who pay their workers to produce those parts...

Money Multiplier

The salesperson and the factory worker need to pay income taxes, and they may decide to save some money instead of buying another product. But the example has served its purpose. By borrowing money to purchase the truck, the original consumer has transferred wealth to others. That original loan has resulted in a multiplier effect, and the economic boom continues as money changes hands.

The money multiplier concept is often associated with Keynesian economic theory, and has been the rationale for using increased government spending or tax cuts to stimulate the U.S. economy. The example given earlier follows this same theory:

Increased consumer spending is followed by an increase in business revenues. Those revenues result in more jobs which once again result in more spending - and so the cycle continues."..........

The concern is understandable: when the Fed signaled in 2013 that the end of its quantitative-easing (QE) policy was forthcoming, the resulting "taper tantrum" sent shockwaves through many emerging countries' financial markets and economies.

Indeed, rising interest rates in the US and the ensuing likely rise in the value of the dollar could, it is feared, wreak havoc among emerging markets' governments, financial institutions, corporations, and even households. Because all have borrowed trillions of dollars in the last few years, they will now face an increase in the real local-currency value of these debts, while rising US rates will push emerging markets' domestic interest rates higher, thus increasing debt-service costs further.

But, although the prospect of the Fed raising interest rates is likely to create significant turbulence in emerging countries' financial markets, the risk of outright crisis and distress is more limited.

Debt is an unwelcome guest at the table in many American households. The average U.S. household with debt carries $15,355 in credit card debt and $129,579 in total debt. The psychology behind debt, as well as its cost, it became clear that increasing debt loads aren't just a result of irresponsible spending. There are many factors at play in the increasing amount of debt being carried in homes across the country. It's easy to say we should simply pay off our balances and free ourselves of the burdens — financial and emotional — that come with financing many aspects of our lives. But it's not that simple.

Some may argue that higher spending will put the economy on a positive track, and to an extent this is true, but consumers shouldn't **sacrifice their wealth just for the sake of economy**. Higher debt levels means more interest paid, which diverts the cash flows from more useful forms. Consumers making large monthly interest payments on their credit cards debt, and this only hurts their financial future in the long run. Consumers should focus on **paying down credit card debt** instead of increasing their spending. Bringing down the amount of overall debt in our nation should be our number one concern.

Imbalances in the global flows of trade and capital* were at the heart of most major economic crises in recent years. In the euro zone, an imbalance between surplus countries like Germany and debtor countries like Greece, Italy and Spain triggered a devastating and ongoing economic crisis. In the U.S. financial crisis, huge inflows of capital helped feed an asset bubble in the housing market that eventually popped, impoverishing millions of American families.

For one, the current debate ignores the fact that countries can amass trade and current account surpluses through a variety of methods, not just fiddling with the value of their currencies. Any measure that affects the international price of exports can have the same effects.

Some economists argue that China and Germany built up their surpluses in part by holding down worker wages. Tax breaks and direct subsidies for domestic companies can artificially cheapen the cost of exports, as can subsidizing the resources or capital that domestic companies use as inputs. If a country has a floating currency and independent monetary policy, quantitative easing can accomplish the same goal – by expanding the monetary supply, lowering the cost of the currency, and boosting exports. Tellingly, the AAPC proposal originally accused Japan of currency manipulation through quantitative easing, apparently overlooking the fact that the Fed has expanded its balance sheet through QE by $3.6 trillion since late 2008.

WTO and IMF rules prohibit some of these practices, but not all of them. You can certainly argue that some of these behavior are more unfair than others, but whether they are punished depends mostly on who is writing the rules.

Because there are so many moving parts in the cost of exports, efforts to focus on the currency sometimes fail to achieve the desired effect. As Mireya Solis of Brookings writes, "Currency realignment is not a magic pill to eliminate trade deficits." She points out that shifts in the value of the Chinese currency had only marginal effects on the U.S. trade deficit with China, while the sizable depreciation of the dollar against the yen during 2000s did little to reduce the U.S. trade deficit with Japan.

One of the big challenges that we face is that the market outcomes, even in relatively high-performing economies—that is, high performing relative to their stage of development — are turning out to be pretty seriously out of whack. And this is different from the early postwar period.

In the early postwar period, things looked pretty good, you know? The advanced countries grew well. The war-damaged countries came along. The distributional effects were pretty benign. The middle class grew—opportunity abounded. The developing countries started to grow, and so on.

Now we're in a situation in which the income and wealth distributions are skewing the other way. The share of labour income in total income is declining. There's less optimism. There's very high unemployment in pockets of poor economic performances in Europe. So it looks like there are forces at work that are making a sort of growth, you know, GDP diverge from the employment patterns.

Poverty is something every human detest and dislikes the most, yet, poverty shameless likes to stick along with as many people it possibly could manage to be with, none of us human like to stay in poverty, Sex, money and power; is what each of us desire to obtain, Power of money is arguably the most desired power a person would like to have, we all love to be rich and wealthy, but very few fortunate individuals succeeds in obtaining wealth and lives happy healthy and wealthy life.

Here have listen to this, **"Money is no God – but, money is no less than God,"** **money is not everything in life but our life is nothing without money.**

Indeed money is the most significant and prominent requirement of every human, we need money every step of the way in our life, for Food, clothes, housing and education, we people simply can't survive without money, but yet there are billions who are surviving with very little money in their hands to spend.

Staggering 60% of global population falls under lower income category, India and China are the two most populous nations in the world, therefore not surprising maximum number of poor as well live in these two countries, India perhaps is the worst affected of the two, when it comes to measuring income and purchasing power, astounding figures according to estimates 380 million Indians are **acutely**

poor, and in China nearly 400 million Chinese are categorised as low earning or lower income families or individuals.

What are those uncanny reasons for such high level of poverty in our world? There are wide variety and combination of factors and reasons for staggeringly high level of poverty in our world, some of the key reasons for increased poverty in world are, mismanagement of resources, terrorism, protracted and sustain wars, insurgency and civil wars in many countries around the world, corruption in high places, frequent natural disasters and also demographic problems. Such examples and reasons of poverty and inequality are no doubt real. But there are other deeper and more profound reasons for chronic global poverty which apparently are not discussed.

Brutal wars and violence, criminal activities and gun violence, also natural disasters and freak road accidents, railways and industrial accidents claims millions of lives annually, across the globe millions of people die unnatural and untimely deaths, and what is even more disheartening fact is, that, majority of people who die in violence or accidents are mostly young people below the age of 40, and even bigger worrisome reality is that many of these folks who die are the sole bread winner of their family, the world is losing young talented demographic, if so many young men and women lose their lives prematurely, and many among these young men and women are principle earning member of their respective families, so when they die or are seriously injured and wounded it leaves their family without any viable source of income, this in turn creates more fundamental social and economic problems.

Globally there is serious health-care and demographic problems, demographic challenges are far too many, different countries have different demographic problems, while rich industrialized nations like Germany and Japan have growing percentage of elderly population, also China because of its more than three decades long strict One child policy, however China did relax its one child policy beginning of year 2016, and has allowed parents an option of having a second child if they want to, however enough damage has already been done, China as well like many European countries have rising elderly population. While many wealthy and prosperous nations of world have large elderly population, it is the opposite in many underdeveloped and poor countries, in India for instance has significantly high younger demographic, according to some surveys as of 2014 60% of India's population is/was below the age of 35, similarly in Pakistan, Bangladesh and many other Islamic countries like Turkey and Egypt etc have huge younger population, so it is a major challenge and difficulty for the countries which have large younger population, such countries desperately struggles hard to serve interest of their respective country's large younger demographic, to provide good education and healthcare to youngsters is always a challenge for the government of any country, and even more difficult is to create new job and business opportunities for younger demographic.

Have rare insight and broader perspective for growing demographic problems particularly in developed western countries, falling fertility rates, many modern fashionable feminist White European women and also modern Black African women in 21st century have become more career oriented, preferring to focus more on developing professional career rather than to start their own family and become mother, so delaying marriage and differing pregnancy, postponing motherhood for considerably longer period of time, most White European or even Black African modern day women you'll see becomes mother for the first time only after they've celebrated their 30th birthday.

But in stark contrast to White European and Black African women, you'll see it that majority of Muslim girls and women at the time when they celebrate their 25th birthday they are already mother of 3 or 4 children, large population of Muslim community is socio-culturally conservative and do not adopt family planning methods, it is highly likely that average Muslim women even if she is working yet she will get married at early age and will not delay pregnancy, so it is not surprising that Muslim population percentage wise as compare to every other religious communities grows faster, birth rate within Muslims community is very high.

But there's another perspective as well with regards to global Muslim population, it is true that for past many years and decades Muslims are scoring higher points in terms of birth rate, but not many have observed another reality that the mortality rate or death rate among Muslims is high as well, it has been observe that Muslim women outlives Muslim men, life expectancy of Muslim women is higher than Muslim men, why? There are some ridiculously odd reasons as to why the death rate among Muslim is high, it is because in most of the Islamic rule countries in the world or Muslim dominated countries have nerve-wrecking history as well as ongoing reality of destructive wars and civil wars, besides have higher degree of terrorist attacks and communal violence, also some of the Islamic countries are prone to frequent natural disasters (earthquakes, tsunamis or floods) and extreme weather conditions (treacherous heat waves or extreme cold weather), so all these combination of reasons and factors are responsible for claiming many lives, considerably large number of Muslims particularly in Muslim dominated countries dies in wars and terrorists related or other form of brutal fights and violence. But despite so many Muslims dying unnatural death in violence and or due to harsh weather conditions, yet as of 2015 the world's Muslim population remains 1.6 billion strong.

Now to eradicate poverty it is necessary that all of us need to have stable source of monthly income, especially younger demographic crave for better quality jobs and professional or business opportunities, but, are there enough jobs available? What's on offer? No dear, new age modern technology is creating few jobs and destroying more jobs, Internet revolution has helped in creating and developing many sophisticated devices and software, 21st century technology also called Artificial intelligence, so availability of Automated machines, Industrial robots and robotic technology, then upgradation of cloud computing technology, once industries and businesses deploys these available apparatus and newly developed or upgraded software applications, they then don't need large staff or employees, instead businesses can reduce their workforce because few talented employees is all that's required who all can do lot more work, so robotic technology and cloud computing technology immensely helps businesses reduce overheads requirements, just few employees needed and those few employees will be able to do lot more work thereby reducing expenditure of companies and substantially increasing productivity.

Most parents still believe that there children needs to have high quality education that will ultimately help their children establish themselves and will secure their future, many parents especially in Asia and in Africa but particularly in Indian sub-continent countries still believe in sending their children especially their son/sons to best possible schools, college and university because they firmly believe that once their son completes university studies and get a university Master's degree or diploma certificate that will help him get high paying corporate job and there also is another intimate reason as well since many conservative Asian parents thinks and imagine that once their son have higher educational degrees and good job that will help him get suitable bride and higher dowry amount, and to ensure their son/sons get best possible academic qualification, most parents in case if they don't have sufficient financial resources they do not hesitate one bit in selling their valuables or borrowing money from their friends and relatives. Well most people prefer to go by their perception but there are very few who do reality check before making choices and taking decisions.

Unemployment is a problem but underemployment is another bigger problem, for most people in our world it doesn't matter what field or sector they have to work in, they simply want a job to earn money, they accept any job that comes their way, but there are some individual people who are very particular about what job they need and would like doing, and they never compromise on their interest, for example, if a young man has done hotel management and or catering course and have a degree, he will only prefer working in hospitality or related industry but he under no circumstances would accept job in other non-matching or unrelated industries or sector.

This is what is major problem many youngsters around the world experience, want a job desperately but there aren't enough jobs available and those jobs that are available are not suitable and many find it below their dignity to do such kinds of jobs, but again we need to come to terms with reality and have limited choice or are left with no choice at all because after all we all have to pay our monthly bills.

Many university pass degree holders unable to find a job that matches their talent despite paying huge amounts to get a higher education, circumstances forces them to take lower-skilled job "elementary occupation" job such as "office junior, hospital porters, waiters, bartenders roads sweeper, window cleaner or shelf stackers," now when highly educated men and women starts doing such low skilled jobs despite being degree holders this will in turn pushes out those who don't have a degree out of job market altogether.

Young people are simply not getting the opportunities they deserve. If we don't create better jobs for graduates we won't be able to build the higher-skilled workforce needed so desperately to boost global business productivity.

College and Universities cost thousands of dollars a semester, not including books, room, and board. Tuition has gone up 1,120 percent in the last thirty years. Students have been given the impression that employers are looking for people who, through test and grades, have showed that they are high achievers. In many recent surveys, that has been proved otherwise. Employers are looking for people who have learned how to learn and have gained substantial communication skills, as well as critical thinking abilities. Graduates aren't meeting the employers needs. Students are also strongly struggling with paying off their student loans. Without the desired, and needed jobs, graduates are building debt and struggling to pay back their debt. 15 percent of the student borrowers default within the first three years of repayment. Many resort back to living at home and having to work multiple part-time jobs. Loans average about twenty to thirty thousand dollars. Higher education becomes an investment in which students are expecting to find a job with enough income to pay off the loans in a timely manner.

At 7or 8% annual growth, the China's labour market will generate about eight million jobs, but these jobs if created will mainly be in manufacturing industries and requirement will be low-level qualifications but high level of technical and mechanical skills.

Fast growing East Asian economies have rapidly increased the numbers of students attending university in recent years. Now the pool of unemployed graduates is rising to worrying levels in the region generally – and even in some high-growth economies. Of particular concern is whether high graduate unemployment is a temporary blip or reflects a chronic oversupply of graduates, even as many employers say they cannot find people with the right skills. Experts stress that Asian countries need to focus not just on expanding higher education but also ensuring quality at the same time if graduate unemployment is to be contained.

In South Korea the number of 'economically inactive' graduates has passed three million for the first time, according to government figures released in February-2014, up just over 3% from the previous year. South Korea has among the highest university participation rates in the world, at around 80% compared with 15% to 40% for most advanced economies and below 15% for most developing countries in Asia. "The main reason (for rising joblessness) is that there is a growing number of college graduates.

Critical thinking and problem solving, for example, have been components of human progress throughout history, from the development of early tools, to agricultural advancements, to the invention of vaccines, to land and sea exploration. Such skills as information literacy and global awareness are not new, at least not among the elites in different societies. The need for mastery of different kinds of knowledge, ranging from facts to complex analysis? Not new either. In *The Republic*, Plato wrote about four distinct levels of intellect. Perhaps at the time, these were considered "3rd century BCE skills"?

What's actually new is the extent to which changes in our economy and the world mean that collective and individual success depends on having such skills. Many U.S. students are taught these skills—those who are fortunate enough to attend highly effective schools or at least encounter great teachers—but it's a matter of chance rather than the deliberate design of our school system. Today we cannot afford a system in which receiving a high-quality education is akin to a game of bingo. If we are to have a more equitable and effective public education system, skills that have been the province of the few must become universal.

This distinction between "skills that are novel" and "skills that must be taught more intentionally and effectively" ought to lead policymakers to different education reforms than those they are now considering. If these skills were indeed new, then perhaps we would need a radical overhaul of how we think about content and curriculum. But if the issue is, instead, that schools must be more deliberate about teaching critical thinking, collaboration, and problem solving to all students, then the remedies are more obvious, although still intensely challenging.

The history of U.S. education reform should greatly concern everyone who wants schools to do a better job of teaching students to think. Many reform efforts, from reducing class size to improving reading instruction, have devolved into fads or been implemented with weak fidelity to their core intent. The 21st century skills movement faces the same risk.

To complicate the challenge, some of the rhetoric we have heard surrounding this movement suggests that with so much new knowledge being created, content no longer matters; that ways of knowing information are now much more important than information itself. Such notions contradict what we know about teaching and learning and raise concerns that the 21st century skills movement will end up being a weak intervention for the very students—low-income students and students of colour—who most need powerful schools as a matter of social equity.

Read couple of paragraph from Book "**HOW TO CREATE WEALTH: POWER OF MONEY**" "Some other reasons, why this world is ridden by poverty is because of structural discriminations and systematic bias, gender discrimination particularly against females, still living with primitive era mind-set, many ethnic and religious communities are yet reluctant to adopt modern norms and modern style of living, socially conservative religious communities do not allow their daughters the freedom to step out of there house and explore the world, explore to seize an opportunities to become career oriented, many fanatics in some religious communities do not allow their women and girls to make career in Singing, dancing acting, sports or to become fashion models, so as a result of which millions of girls outrageously remains in confinement of their house and under close observation of elder members of their community, so, this is how, many women and girls are deprived of the opportunities to manifest their charm and prove their abilities.

Language becomes another hurdle in progress of many youths, also, linguistic chauvinism becomes stumbling-block in social and economic development of some countries. English is De facto a world's language, as, English is widely spoken and most preferred and understood language in the world, apart from English there are few other languages as well which are spoken and understood by more than Billion people around the world, languages like Hindi and Mandarin are couple of other most popular languages, while Hindi and Urdu language is spoken and understood in major parts of the Indian sub-continent and other Asian countries and Mandarin is a Chinese language spoken and understood by over billion people in China and other far eastern Asian countries, apart from these Three widely spoken languages there are other languages as well like French, Spanish and German which are as well considerably popular languages.

We learn to speak multiple languages perhaps not because we love that particular language/languages but we learn languages to connect with people from other parts of the world, for trade and commerce purpose, to understand different cultures and civilizations by communicating with people from different religions and regions of the world, but there apparently are folks in many countries from different communities and ethnic groups who are unrelenting, they do not like learning languages other than their own language (which they consider as their Mother tongue) as they fear that if they learn to speak English, Hindi or Mandarin or any other national languages in such case there young generation will stop communicating among themselves in their own language, hence their language which they relate it to their culture will lose identity. It is a "Strategic Blunder" on part of those who hold such linguistic prejudice because not learning multiple languages especially the dominating languages of the world which are spoken and understood by over billion people, most people seriously and comprehensively lose out on opportunities in life because one reason is that their own country perhaps may be debt ridden impoverish nation and may not provide good enough jobs and business opportunities and other reason because of Language Barrier they will always find it difficult to blend themselves with folks from other communities and countries.

Linguistic prejudice potentially holds back the progress and development of countries and their demographics." Article Sourced from Book "**How to Create Wealth: Power of Money.**"........................

In a capitalist economy, the political system emphasizes competition for resources as a means of increasing capital (or wealth) and developing personal success. In a socialist economy, the emphasis is on distributing wealth so that individual needs are met with collective capital. There are many different versions of both capitalism and socialism, and most modern societies are a blend of the two. Americans are known to be risk takers and capital makers. In the US it is possible to begin a business of humble means and expand it to grow into a conglomerate business model for people wanting to start a new business. Imagine a tiny dry cleaner who adds space in strip malls and soon owns over twenty **businesses**. This is the epitome of wealth and capitalism in the US. Capitalism in the US has no colour and welcomes anyone willing to work hard, market a product and to bring it to fruition. Whereas German industries have prospered because the country has made it a priority to train its labour force to succeed in various industries. These various systems have worked together to make a robust capitalistic market for the country. The **German model** of prosperity supports allowing local entrepreneurs to develop and initiate new industries which help the people to communicate better with the world and to meet their needs in becoming current world players in the technology industries.

Here to have a better perspective of the two main political and economic system **Capitalism** and **Socialism** which are principle system that most of the countries across the world use or have adopted to govern their respective country, I would like to share excerpts from article "Capitalism & Socialism: Two Old Economic Visions" Theories, we are often told, are merely abstractions with no real practical impact, but hardly anything has impacted modern history more profoundly than capitalism and socialism. ~ Riane Eisler, The Real Wealth of Nations

For most of recorded history, whether Eastern or Western, the vast majority of people were poor, and, as they had been taught to do, accepted poverty as their inevitable lot. But as the industrial revolution gained steam in Europe, so did the possibility that the world can change. By the middle 1700s, the vision of progress through human intervention was applied to economics. If people could improve the means of production, perhaps they could also improve the economic system. With a better understanding of how economic systems function, we could make them work for the greater good of all.

Out of this new probing of economic patterns, two economic theories emerged. The first theory described what we today call capitalism. The second theory is what its proponents called socialism.

Theories, we are often told, are merely abstractions with no real practical impact, but hardly anything has impacted modern history more profoundly than capitalism and socialism. Understanding these theories and the times out of which they came is key to recognizing the dominator assumptions embedded in them, and to building a new economic theory called *partnerism* – one that really works for the greater good of all.

The Capitalist Vision

Adam Smith (born in Scotland in 1723) wrote his famous *Inquiry into the Nature and Cases of the Wealth of Nations* in 1776, the same year the United States was born. Smith's book, better known simply as *The Wealth of Nations*, became the "bible" of capitalist theory. Smith's was an optimistic vision of the future. He basically accepted the dominator belief that people are inherently selfish. But in his view, this selfishness could work for the common good – if only the market was left to regulate production and commerce without government interference.

Smith wrote in a time of massive social and economic dislocation. The gentry had appropriated most of the lands that were commons, and hordes of dispossessed farmers reduced to paupers were roaming the countryside. There were also already signs of what was to come with the advent of full-fledged 19th century industrialization. In some places, young children worked in mines 12 hours a day as did women, including pregnant women, who sometimes gave birth in mine shafts. Conditions in some manufacturing towns weren't much better, with children tending machines round the clock for twelve to fourteen hours at a stretch.

The Socialist Vision

In important respects, capitalism was a step forward in the move from a dominator to a partnership way of life. It gave impetus to more socially accountable political forms, such as constitutional monarchies and republics, and was a major factor in the creation of a middle class. Certainly capitalism was preferable to the earlier feudal and mercantile economic systems in which nobles and kings owned most economic resources.

However, capitalism emphasized individual acquisitiveness and greed (the profit motive), relied on rankings (the class structure), continued traditions of violence (colonial conquests and wars), and failed to recognize the economic importance of the "women's work" of caring and caregiving. In these and other ways, capitalism retained significant dominator elements.

By the 19th century, when it was clear that capitalism was not fulfilling Smith's vision of an economics that works for the common good, Karl Marx and Friedrich Engels proposed a very different theory. Theirs was to be known as scientific socialism, and it challenged just about everything Smith had believed – particularly his faith in the forces of the market.

Marx's and Engels' scientific socialism was an alternative to what they dismissed as the utopian socialism of theorists such as Robert Owen and Charles Fourier. Marx and Engels believed that class conflicts are historically inevitable, and that the victory of the bourgeoisie or merchant class over the feudal landed aristocracy would inevitably be followed by the victory of the working class or proletariat. But they were not only committed to constructing a new economic theory; they were also committed to seeing it put into action.

In time, Marx's and Engels' dream of a successful communist revolution was realized. But not in an industrialized capitalist nation, as they had predicted. Instead, revolution came in an agricultural semi-feudal society: the Russia of autocratic tsars and nobles.

Although socialist policies ended mass hunger and destitution and vastly improved healthcare and education, traditions of domination in both the family and state did not change. What Marx called the dictatorship of the proletariat turned into just that – another violent and despotic regime.

The central planners created a top-down form of state capitalism where resources were controlled by a small group of men from the top. In Moscow, government apparatniks got perks such as seaside villas and sumptuous banquets, while the mass of people lived in overcrowded flats and often lacked staple foods. In the provinces, warlords became communist commissars and continued to terrorize their people.

Part of the problem lay in communist theory itself. Not only did it dictate the abolition of private property and class warfare; it also failed to abandon the dominator tenet that violence is the means to power, as in the well-known adage "The end justifies the means." But an even bigger part of the problem was the rigid dominator nature of the culture that preceded the Soviet Union.".................

The reason for disharmony in our society and main cause for why it's so prevalent is because of rising religious intolerance in civil society around the world, widespread communal and religious strife and violence, religious prejudice is worse type of prejudice, and the reason for growing religious intolerance is because large majority of people have inadequate and incomprehensible or absolutely Zero knowledge and understanding of various different religions and sub-religious caste and communities that exist in our world, overwhelmingly large majority of people do not have any meaningful detail information and understanding of various different culture and civilizations, "People around the World become victim of propaganda, it is because most of the people are **NOT** Intellectually Competent." Intellectually bankrupt people lacks majorly in having any sort of comprehensive knowledge and understanding of greater and deeper worldly matters and issues, that's because maximum number of people around the world do not read scientific and philosophical literature, people think it's boring reading philosophical and scientific literature, and because of erroneous belief most people around the world commits enormous errors in dealing with many seriously important day to day matters and issues.

Wisdom helps us avoid making mistakes, having a perspective, challenging our perspective help us take appropriate and correct decisions in life.

To solve our problems and to avoid unnecessary hassle and problems in our life, we need to have *Critical thinking skills* which eventually will help us develop Analytical skills, so reading scientific and philosophical literature may help us gain knowledge and wisdom. Having educational degrees and certificates or not having degrees, it doesn't make any significant difference, a person becomes **Intelligent** when he/she is determined to apply his/her mind to learn new things, ready to alter their thoughts and make required changes wherever its necessary.

It perhaps may not be possible to eradicate poverty but if global leaders and policy makers take some sincere and pragmatic steps and if bold measures are taken and if global leaders adopts positive attitude then there is every chance poverty can considerably be alleviated.

Create economic value and don't destroy economic value, there is lot of value in value additions, business owners should always try to add value to the product they produce that will help their business grow significantly and become more productive and therefore earn substantially more profits.

Many resource dependant countries are inadvertently or to say rather brazenly losing big opportunity to earn higher amount of cash revenue, therefore depriving their nation's treasury as well their respective country's citizens from obtaining wealth.

If a country is fortunate enough to have naturally available natural resources, in which case that fortunate country should apply business common sense to make extensive use and take optimal advantage of available resources, and should not diminish or devalue their advantage and giveaway benefits to others to derive maximum gain, whether it is soft commodity or hard commodity, if for example in a country where there is large production of Milk, Now Milk is something which is an ingredient as well as raw material to make hundreds of items, so instead of just selling entire production of Milk in raw form, if manufacturing facilities are created and factories and industries are set up to manufacture high value added products like Ice-creams, flavoured Milk shakes, flavoured yogurt, butter, cheese, and then sold in open markets or exported, similarly if a country which produces large quantity of Cocoa Beans, Cocoa beans is arguably the most precious agri-commodity, hundreds of delicious food products are made using cocoa beans as ingredient or raw material, so if the country which is fortunate to have large production of cocoa beans, now doesn't it make sense for that country to use entire production of cocoa beans domestically and for that purpose to have manufacturing industrial units in their own country so as to manufacture high-end value added products like Cakes, chocolates, biscuits, ice-creams etc and then selling it in open market or to export it to foreign countries, just imagine how much value can be added and how much more revenue can be generated but more important so much more wealth can be created and thereby upgrade and improve standard of living of their citizens and adding excitement to the country's economy.

Similarly in case of hard commodity, there are few countries in the world which possesses abundant reserves of minerals and crude oil & gas, for example if a country that have large reserves of iron-ore, copper or bauxite, instead of exporting iron-ore or bauxite in raw form, if upstream industries are set up in their own country, and use available minerals as raw material to manufacture high-end value added Iron and steel and Aluminium products, also if countries which have vast reserves of petroleum crude oil, so these countries need to create large manufacturing facilities in their own country set up large Petrochemical industries and Refineries to processes entire crude oil production and then sell it in open market or export high end value added petroleum products like Speciality chemicals, ethylene, jet fuel oil, and auto fuel.

Australia, Russia, Brazil, Canada, Norway, Saudi Arabia, Iran and Iraq are some among many countries rich in natural resources, these are some of the most prominent countries which have formidable deposits of various different types of minerals and petroleum oil & gas, but these countries have for years and decades have recklessly and senselessly been selling minerals like "Iron-ore, coal, copper, zinc, bauxite and of course petroleum oil and gas" in crude raw form, so, who benefits? Countries like India, China, South-Korea and European countries are major beneficiaries, factory owners and industries in several European countries and also in India and China have been sourcing industrial commodities like Iron-ore, zinc, copper and more importantly the most sensitive commodity of all petroleum crude oil and gas, and have been using these sourced mineral commodities as raw material to manufacture hundreds of different types and kinds of value added products and have been making enormous profits.

Sparkling stones as we call it Diamonds, principle producing countries like Botswana and South-Africa exports uncut raw rough diamonds and particularly to one country that's to India, in India Diamond traders and merchants sources rough diamonds in raw form, than they cut and polish diamonds to precise sizes and further adds value to it, by using gold and diamonds to make fancy and fashionable ornaments and jewellery and then sells it thru retail outlets to buyers or exports at unbelievably high prices, so this is how Indian diamond merchants have been earning millions of U.S-dollars.

This is how perhaps for generations resource rich nations have been losing big amount of money, because all these years simply selling or exporting naturally available resources in raw form at a giveaway prices, these inept resource rich nations are simply destroying economic value of their country, and these counties economic policy planners economists and politicians are shamelessly depriving millions of their country's citizens an opportunity to work in highly complex industrial units and earn big amount of money, and millions of citizens of these badly managed resource rich countries are losing big time opportunities to become rich and wealthy.

Sharp volatility in resource (commodities) prices makes resource rich countries economy more unstable, what adds to the problem is the role of strategic investors, international financial institutions, commercial banks and hedge-fund investors **rush in** to invest big amount of money when commodity prices are higher, and **rush out** of the country when commodity prices are declining, abrupt flow in and flow out of large amount of foreign money, all of which causes instability in both stock-markets and currency markets, such high uncertainty about economic growth, that's precisely the reason, why you'll find much higher unemployment in most of the natural resource rich countries.

Good politics brings about excellent economic gains for any country, and bad politics destroys economic value of a country.

Right in the beginning of 21st century, in immediate aftermath of 9/11 terror attacks on U.S soil, the then incumbent U.S president Mr George W Bush, with great determination started **"War on Terror,"** the purpose of starting a war on terror was not only for U.S to seek revenge against its enemies but also in larger global interest to help world's population get rid from the menace of extremists and religious terrorism. But, there are some pressing questions which needs answers, did this "war on terror" achieved its desired objective? Has the U.S and its allies army succeeded in dismantling the Sunni Muslim Jihadists terror network and degrading the terrorist force combative and striking capacity and abilities? What did U.SA the world's leading superpower nation achieved from launching global **war on terror**? The answers for all above questions is "**absolutely nothing**," the U.S inspired and financed war on terror has simply proven to be directionless unending protracted war, which has no end in sight, with regards to world becoming more safe, no *not at all* in fact in years 2013 and 2015 the world has become more unsafe and dangerous place to live in. on the contrary the Sunni-Muslim jihadist terrorists have gained considerably more strength and combative power.

It is only hot rhetoric, war on terror has proved to be mere war of words and very little substance, the world heavyweight political leaders use aggressive tone and speaks profoundly powerful language and assures to public their resolve of defeating the radical Sunni jihadists forces, but it all seems phony aggression and false commitments, all words no real action on ground. By any means do a reality check and you'll find that Sunni terrorists groups have gained enormous strength over the past few years, terrorist related violence between 2013 and 2015 has reached all time high and with no respite in sight from terrorism and religious intolerance, analysts expects violence to get more nasty in coming years.

Islamic terrorists forces have significantly strengthen their support base and combative capabilities, the war on terror was started in 2001, but since then the Islamic army or call them terrorists forces have become more organized and have institutionalised their operation, so with regards to much hyped War on Terror, who gained and who have lost thus far? Definitely common-people have not benefited anything but have lost many things. But few crafty politicians made political capital out of it by taking undue advantage of growing islamophobia in many prominent countries, some astute politicians systematically polarized their political constituency and won elections and succeeded in occupying highest political office of their country. But not only non-Islamic politicians who have gained also many politicians and government officials of Muslim ruled states have also in many ways immensely profited from rising terrorists activities in their country or in their region.

The officially declared war which U.S fought first in Afghanistan in 2001 and later in Iraq in 2003 has cost over One Trillion U.S-Dollar, between 2001 and 2015 in Afghanistan and Iraq alone at least One million people including soldiers and so-called jihadi terrorists may have lost their lives, thousands of U.S army personnel and soldiers and other officials are/were either killed and died, and thousands more who were seriously wounded and injured and as result of injuries many among them have/had become physically challenged.

With trillions of dollar of expenditure incurred for fighting wars and fighting against the terrorists and insurgent armies in various Islamic countries in Asia and Africa, some more individual people and corporates may have profited, yes, indeed, the defence contractors, arms dealers, arms and ammunition manufacturing companies and defence equipment suppliers have all made oodles of money, not to forget corrupt politicians and government officials in several Islamic countries affected by terrorism and civil wars as well have immensely benefited. It was initially said before the start of war on terror, that, this war on terror is to serve Human Purpose, but as things have unravel, the facts began to surface, it has become evident that the war on terror has actually served and fulfilled purpose of egocentric self-seeking individuals and businessmen and above all served Commercial Interest.

With regards to U.S spending Trillions of Dollars on War on Terror, instead U.S government officials and ruling administration would had been better advised had U.S instead of spending Trillions fighting wars in Iraq and Afghanistan and then expanding war on terror to other Islamic countries in the Persian gulf region, had U.S used this trillions of dollars at home on repairing and upgrading existing infrastructure and developing new infrastructure and used money on providing healthcare benefits to its citizens, all these expenditure would have helped create millions of jobs in all of north-America and would have helped accelerate growth of domestic industry in U.S.

There is a famous saying "Politics makes strange bedfellows," politicians also have brazen double standards, America's staunchest ally in the west-Asia is none other than Saudi Arabia, now Americans and European politicians and intellectual class talks a lot and delivers emotional speeches condemning human rights abuses and favours freedom of speech and civil liberties, and pleads for social justice for all, but strangely enough U.S strongest ally the Saudis are arguably the worst human rights abuser with brutal track record of suppression of its citizens particularly targeting minorities and women.

Not only that Saudi Arabia is ferocious offender of human rights, but is also responsible for committing genocide inside its neighbouring impoverish country **Yemen**, Saudi is one of the world's leading importer of arms and ammunitions, Saudi purchases most of its military hardware and ammunitions from Britain, U.S. and perhaps also from France, Saudi army ostensibly has been using British made weapons to target Shia Houthis inside Yemen and according to some estimates Saudi Arabia's army between 2014/15 is responsible for killing 6,000 Shias most of those killed are/were civilians in Yemen, flouting all international convention and rules, while Saudi Arabia is committing barbaric war crimes killing mainly civilian population and destroying infrastructure and properties worth hundreds of millions dollar, and the greatest advocates of human rights and social justice, the French, British and Germans are merely staring at events happening inside Yemen, maintaining stoic silence not a word of condemnation or expression of solidarity with Shia community, Sunni Islamic folks supresses the minority Shia community and western countries disgracefully ignores cruel atrocities committed against Shiite population.

Not just the Saudis but another devout western ally the Israelis as well are doing there bit to allegedly help the Sunni jihadists, Israel often targets key Shiite army bases and installation in Syria and Lebanon to allegedly help Sunni insurgent jihadi army consolidate their position inside Syria, also it has been reported as well has been witnessed that many of the seriously injured and wounded Al Qaeda and Al Nusra front terrorists when they suffer injuries or are wounded many of these wounded jihadists allegedly receives medical care and treatment in Israeli hospitals.

With regards to Syrian civil war, it is alleged that initially at the start of civil war in Syria in 2011/12 many incidents of killing innocent civilians and massacres were strategically planned and committed by pro-western and Saudi backed jihadists and systematically blamed pro government Syrian army for all the killings to defame and to denigrate secular Syrian president Bashar al-Assad.

Hot rhetoric but soft action, we see and listen American, French, British and many other countries politicians delivering aggressive hard hitting speeches against the so-called Radical Islamist jihadists, and in strongly worded language **vows** and **pledges** before their people that they'll not rest until the moment they destroy Sunni Islamic terror network and decimate jihadi terrorism, well this are all talk, **War on terror** --- on ground there is very little action mere academic or to say un-pragmatic fight against Sunni terrorism, be it in Afghanistan, Iraq or Syria, western army action is over-reported in media while in real term very little happens on the battle ground. Prominent Sunni jihadi forces are or have gained immense strength and No western army or any other significantly strong armed forces are sincerely trying to stop the menace of Islamic terror, no one daring to hunt them out and destroy Sunni terrorist groups who are spread in so many different parts of Asia and in Africa, Somalia based Al – Shabaab incredibly powerful terrorist outfit in east-Africa, Nigeria based Boko Haram arguably the most dreaded terrorist group, besides Nigeria Boko Haram terrorists terrorizes in many other countries in west and central Africa, Afghanistan based Radical Sunni terrorist group Taliban has become more stronger than it ever was between 2012 and 2015, so apart from *ISIS and Al Qaeda* there are many Sunni terrorist groups who are ferociously and frivolously carrying out terrorist activities, unrestrictedly terrorizing and humiliating innocent civilians, but no army or security forces *"worth its salt"* have genuinely attempted to eliminate these terrorists organizations, Boko Haram, Al Shabaab or Taliban remains largely untouched and unchallenged.

Evidently it is only the Iranian backed Shiite army and other Shiite groups like Shia-Houthis and Hezbollah's army are seen fighting Sunni jihadist terrorists in Iraq, Syria and even in Yemen.

According to historians, it was in June-632AD immediately after the death of the founder of Islam Prophet Mohammed, it is believed Islam got divided into two faction "**Shia and Sunni**," now as per my own understanding about Islamic history, it is for the first time in hundreds of years since Islam got divided into two faction that the Shiites have grouped themselves and they are resolutely opposing

Sunnis highhandedness and vehemently fighting against Sunni terrorism, or else for all these hundreds of years the Sunnis have dominated and have brutally suppressed and battered the beleaguered Shia community.

The dynamics of Middle-East conflict changed and all new dimension was added to Islamic sectarian war in west-Asia when the Russian armed forces threw their weight behind Syrian and Shiite army, long after observing war from safer distance, the Russian army stepped in and completely changed the complexion of war in Arabian countries, sometime in middle of year 2015 the audacious and assiduous incumbent Russian President Vladimir Putin ordered his Airforce commanders to bombard the Sunni terrorists hideouts and camps inside Syria. Russian forces mainly targeting Western and Saudis and Qataris backed jihadists camps, Russia's military response thoroughly irked the western power, the *French, British and Americans* shocked and flabbergast with Russian Airforce action largely targeting jihadist the so-called <u>free Syrian army</u> whom the western power had long been nurturing, training and aiding to fight against Iranian backed army to gain control in the petroleum oil and gas rich west-Asia region, western allies in the west-Asia region Sunni power <u>Saudi Arabia and Turkey</u> as well were jittery and tense by Russian president Putin's bold initiatives and rendering his support to their arch rival and known foe the Shiite army.

"Russia's support for Syria dates back to 1946, when Russia helped consolidate Syria's independence. The two countries mutually came to a diplomatic and military agreement in the form of a non-aggression pact, which was enacted on April 20, 1950. In this pact, Russia promised support to the newly-created Syria by helping to develop its military and by providing tactical support. Essentially, Russia and Syria have been cooperating for decades both militarily and economically, with Russia maintaining a naval base on the Syrian Mediterranean."

Russia's increasingly aggressive posture has sparked a sweeping review among U.S. defence strategists of America's military policies and contingency plans in the event of a conflict with the former Soviet state. With the launch of airstrikes in Syria, Russian President Vladimir Putin instigated a proxy war with the U.S., putting those nation's powerful militaries in support of opposing sides of the multipolar conflict. And it's a huge gamble for Moscow.

Make no mistake: Experts agree that the U.S. military's globe-spanning force would clobber the Russian military in any toe-to-toe conventional fight. But modern wars are not toe-to-toe conventional fights; geography, politics and terrain inevitably give one side an advantage. Today, the U.S. spends nearly 10 times more than Russia on national defence. The U.S. operates 10 aircraft carriers; Russia has just one. And the U.S. military maintains a broad technological edge and a vastly superior ability to project power around the world. Russia remains weak, according to many traditional criteria. But it is now developing some key technologies, new fighting tactics and a brazen geopolitical strategy that is aggressively undermining America's 25-year claim to being the only truly global superpower. The result: Russia has unexpectedly re-emerged as America's chief military rival.

There are extremist elements not just in Islam but in other communities as well, but visibly evident involvement of Sunni Islamist jihadists in Spate of Mass shootings, terror attacks targeting and killing innocent helpless civilians in many different parts of the world, and gruesome beheadings of many kidnapped western hostage by ISIS, frequent involvement of Sunni-Islamic folks in barbaric crimes against humanity has stigmatized the Sunni-Muslim community but worse still has world over given phenomenal rise to Islamophobia, intense dislike and hatred for Muslims among large section of world's population, the opportunist Far-Right and rightist leaning extremist politicians and hatred mongers, are desperately trying to take advantage of pervasive climate of islamophobia that persist across the world, both sides, pro-Muslims and anti-Muslim forces, the leftist as well as rightist trying to take advantage of anti-Muslim sentiments, hate monger politicians tries to exploit deep division in culturally and religiously polarized society for their personal benefit, the Far-right rightist extremist politicians brainwash particular section of society to further divide civil society and wins elections.

Islamic terrorism and extremism is more flamboyant and candid, hence it is easily recognizable, but there are extremist and self-radicalized individual people in other communities as well, like for example there are extremist and self-radicalized Hindus as well, unlike Islamist terrorists the Hindu terrorism and extremism is more subtle and discreet. Overall the problem with extremism is that no extremist ever is ready to admit or to agree he/she is an extremist, each extremist person have a tendency to plead innocence and to gain sympathy from others.

Talking about Hindu extremism, as Hinduism is majority religion in India, the right wing Hindu political party takes considerable advantage of islamophobia and hate preacher Hindu leaders brainwash naïve and gullible section of Hindu community, and the big section of senseless Hindus believes every nonsense talks of Hindu political leaders and recklessly sympathizes and votes for the Hindus political party, this is how right wing Hindu political party in India wins elections by instilling fears of Islamic terrorism in the minds of Hindu population, Hindu extremist groups always systematically defame Islam by falsely implicating and blaming the Muslims for perpetrated crimes even if those crimes aren't committed by Muslims. So this type of politics is called *divide and rule*. The mainstream media in India is incompetent and inept and largely controlled by fundamentalist Hindu business houses, therefore bias and prejudice media helps causes of right wing Hindu political party by propagating pro-Hindu propaganda.

If we talk of bigger issues in global politics, America being dominant player in international business and political affairs, hence globally those people who are interested in politics and economics takes keen interest in U.S.A's domestic economic and political policies as well as focuses on U.S role in international politics, because U.S is world's largest economy and strongest possible military power in the world, America is often criticize for its foreign policies. For those who study foreign affairs and have been tracking U.S foreign policies will know that U.S foreign policies often harms U.S and more so to the Americans, whether it was U.S involvement in Chinese domestic affairs in the 1930s during Japanese aggression in China, or U.S.A's involvement and indulgence in Korean and Vietnam civil wars was a total fiasco, and of course U.S role in West-Asia and Persian gulf countries internal politics and religious affairs and dealing with Islamic rulers has always been troublesome.

U.S politicians over indulges in Islamic affairs and senselessly involve itself or by default gets involve in Muslim countries civil wars and Islamic internal problems, it is time that U.S. politicians and government administrative officers withdraw themselves from domestic problems of Muslim countries and distance themselves from Islamic religious wars, better leave it to the Muslims to sort out Islamic troubles and let the Arabs and Persians sort out their differences in which so ever possible manner,

It will be better that U.S maintains safe distance from all other regions conflict zones, not just away from Islamic countries but even keep itself away from South-China sea troubles, North-Korea developing nuclear weapons, north-Korea testing Hydrogen Nuclear Bomb and threatening U.S of dire consequences if U.S interferes in Korean matters and if it helps north-Korea's unfriendly neighbouring countries, let the Arabs sought out Islamic problems, Japanese, Koreans and Chinese will sought out their territorial disputes, U.S trying to play dominant role in international affairs is only endangering its own sovereignty and risking life of its own citizens.

It is thought to us that we learn from our past mistakes and never repeat the same mistakes again, but U.S.A didn't learn lesson from Vietnam fiasco, the then U.S. President **Mr George W Bush** in aftermath of 9/11 terror attacks on U.S soil, ordered his army to first attack Afghanistan in 2001 and later invaded Iraq to dislodge from power the brutal Iraqi dictator Saddam, it proved to be a miscalculated move, and created even bigger political and financial mess than Vietnam and Korea had proved to be, it sometime takes time for us to realize our mistakes, so did the Americans, after the loss of thousands of American soldiers lives and incurring Trillions of Dollars in expenses, a decade or so later the

Americans started saying with regret that it was a wrong strategy and a grave strategic blunder for U.S.A to have got involve in Islamic war in Islamic countries, not only the socialists who either way were deeply sceptical about war on terror but even more hardliners the rightists elements in U.S. as well admit it would have been better if U.S.A had not got directly involved in military confrontation with Sunni terrorist army in Afghanistan and Iraq.

U.S politicians and government officials over involvement in overseas affairs has left little or no time it seems to solve ever increasing domestic problems, domestic troubles are mounting at alarming pace in U.S, if we take into account number of deaths in U.S by Islamic terrorists between 2002 and 2015, no more than couple of hundred Americans may have been killed by Sunni jihadists on U.S soil, but what U.S politicians and citizens needs to be more worried about and there only concern should be the brutal rise in killings of innocent Americans in Gun violence, according to estimates each year as many as 30,000 people in U.S.A dies or are killed in Gun violence and by their own home grown terrorists, apart from gun violence there's devastatingly high cases and incidents of racial and religious discrimination and even more troublesome is deteriorating climatic conditions hurricanes, tornados, floods, snow storms and drought. Gosh so much trouble inside U.S, you guys (American folks) in 21st century the U.S politicians better spend more time at home to sort out domestic problems.

So it is not just Islamic wars that world needs to be concern about there are more serious and devastatingly dangerous political issues and problems that threatens global peace and security. In an article **"How Potent are North Korea's threats? – in' BBC;"** has written **"North Korea's threats**

North Korea has frequently employed bellicose rhetoric towards its perceived enemies.

In 1994 South Koreans stocked up on essentials in panic after a threat by a North Korean negotiator to turn Seoul into "a sea of fire" - one which has been repeated several times since.

After US President George W Bush labelled it part of the "axis of evil" in 2002, Pyongyang said it would "mercilessly wipe out the aggressors".

In June 2012 the army warned that artillery was aimed at seven South Korean media groups and threatened a "merciless sacred war".

There is also a pattern of escalating threats whenever South Korea gets a new leader, with misogynist rhetoric directed at South Korea's first female President Park Geun-hye after she was elected in 2013.

While many observers dismiss the rhetoric as bluster, others warn of "the tyranny of low expectations" when it comes to understanding North Korea, because there have been a number of serious regional confrontations.

"If you follow North Korean media you constantly see bellicose language directed against the US and South Korea and occasionally Japan is thrown in there, and it's hard to know what to take seriously. But then when you look at occasions where something really did happen, such as the artillery attack on a South Korean island in 2010, you see there were very clear warnings," Professor John Delury at South Korea's Yonsei university told the BBC.

The North consistently warned that military exercises being conducted in the area would spark a retaliation.
Mr Delury argues that misreading Pyongyang's intentions and misunderstanding its capabilities has kept the US and South Korea **stuck in a North Korean quagmire.**

Picking apart the bluster

In recent years, the North has warned of a pre-emptive nuclear attack on the US in response to the prospect of joint military exercises between South Korea and the US.

"Any time a nation threatens pre-emptive nuclear war, there is cause for concern. North Korea is no exception, with its... shift in rhetoric from accusing the US of imagining a North Korean ballistic missile threat, to vowing to use its ballistic missile capabilities to strike the continental US," says Andrea Berger, from the Royal United Services Institute in London."............

The U.S.A, French, Britain, and Germany's political leaders and government officials have for decades been busily involved in Persian gulf politics and kept themselves occupied with Islamic world's Islamic problems, overindulging in

Muslim dominated countries civil wars and sorting out political and religious dispute, these progressive western countries have solved No problems but have created more problems in Islamic world.

So if the politicians have been involving themselves with Islamic affairs, the business community and also Banking and financial institutions top Executives of rich developed industrialized western countries as well the Japanese business houses have for decades since 1990s been taking keen interest in India's and China's business and economic prospect, the large Multinational corporates and financial institutions from industrialized countries like U.S, Britain, Germany and Japan have invested unprecedented amount of their time and money in India and China,

Over emphasis on growth prospect of India and China by the large Multinational companies and venture capitalists and over investing vast amount of money in these two world's most populous countries, and at the same time not bothering to look for commercial value and business opportunities in other parts of the world, there are many other countries apart from India and China which have significant economic potential yet brazenly been ignored by large multinational companies despite the fact many other countries as well are full of potential and offers excellent business opportunities and chance to make good amount of money.

There are many other promising countries with strong fundamentals, countries like **Iran** for example is land full of opportunities and have lot of scope to become 21st century economic powerhouse, other countries like Ethiopia and Indonesia have excellent business environment and best suited location to do business, then there are countries like Pakistan, Bangladesh and Philippine all these heavily populated countries with large younger demographic are full of potential and are best suited destinations for businesses ideal location for manufacturing and service sector, but there are two region of the world in particular which have lots of potential and have lots to offer to the world in terms of adding superlative value to global economic growth but sadly have been ignored for long time, here I'm talking about entire west-African block of countries and south-America (Latin America), both these region of the world have largely been neglected.

The American and British investment bankers and economists have been traveling to India to give advice to Indian government and corporates as in what measures should to be adopted and how economic and trade policy needs to be planned and implemented to attract foreign investments which will help spur India's economic growth, these economists and financial analysts as well as the merchant bankers and investment bankers instead of wasting their time and money advising Indians, they should have given some of their good advice and suggestions to the U.S government instead, because there are and were some best business and investment opportunities in U.S itself, Americans instead of looking for investment opportunities elsewhere and lecturing others how to grow their respective country's economy have missed out on some spectacular business and investment opportunities in their own country.

From 1995 until 2012 both India and China's economy were growing at steady pace, especially China's economic growth in superfast lane growing at significantly higher rate, but since 2013 China's fast pace economic growth hit a rough patch and considerably slowed down due to wide variety of reasons, emergence of newer low cost producing countries where products can be manufactured at much lower cost, so increase completion from other low cost manufacturers and also increase labour cost in China and factory workers imperious demand causing significant labour unrest, but there is another perspective for Chinese economic slowdown and much bigger problem which is/was climatic problems, as it is that as of 2015 China is world's biggest Greenhouse gas emitter, hence due to toxic air pollution China's government authority had to order many terrible air polluting industrial and manufacturing units to either suspend their production or close there industrial units all to gather. Since China's economic strength is in its manufacturing sector so any upheavals or problems that causes harm to manufacturing industries in China is or was bound to derail China's economic growth, so that's what happened in year 2014/15, also it is alleged that China's banking and financial sector is thoroughly disorganized and inefficient and that was one among many other reason for massive fall in China's stock-markets in 2nd half of 2015.

Similar is the story of economic slowdown in India, India's apparent economic strength was in offering low cost low-end back-office and customer service to overseas clients and customers, but less than satisfactory service of Indian companies and another reason being innovation and upgradation of new age modern technology, like for example Cloud computing technology and innovation of automated machines most of the work nowadays of providing service to customers is done or happens online or new age automated machines helps the customers, hence less manpower required, so in case of India as well emergence of competition from other countries and upgradation of technology has severely impacted India's economic growth prospect. Another reason for India's economy not performing well is because of devastating slowdown in its agriculture sector, India primarily is agri-economy, India's strength once upon a time use to be its agriculture and farming sector, during 1970s and 1980s India's agriculture sector use to grow 7% to 9% annually, but since 2005 India's agriculture sector is performing much below expectation, and is in continuous slump, because of persistent slump in India's agriculture sector it is brutally harming approximately 55% of India's population who all fortunes are either directly or indirectly dependent on agriculture, the reason for declining agriculture sector in India is mostly because of extremely unpredictable weather pattern, there is either drought or extraordinarily excessive rain or unseasonal rains ruins much of the standing crops, so because of considerably large population of India have erratic monthly or annual income, because of economic uncertainty in millions of Indian household therefore consumption demand is not picking up as to the desire levels.

So as per some mathematical calculations both China and India may report that their respective country's GDP is growing at 7% or 8% annually, agree or disagree, but this GDP figures even if it's true perhaps it maybe but the reality is that this reported economic growth is not at all creating new high paying high quality jobs, leave alone talk about high paying even low skill jobs are hard to find in India and China for many of their citizens. And if there is talk about rebalancing and restructuring to transform their economy, when large percentage of your country's working age population are being made redundant or are unable to find new jobs, how than can we expect domestic consumption to rise, when people have no money in their pockets because they don't have suitable job.

Whether its manufacturing sector or services sector, in more competitive business environment, upgradation and innovation of new age technology, **cloud computing and robotic technology** helps businesses and industry become more efficient and productive and requires lot less staff.

Both the two most populous countries India and China aren't able to create enough job opportunities for their younger demographic, so because of lower business confidence and lack of job opportunities, plus high degree of uncertainty over future prospects all combinations of factors have considerably reduced purchasing power of Indians and Chinese. Therefore it was not surprising why demand for luxury items and expensive consumer products on high-street registered steep decline in the year 2015.

The swift pace of China's currency decline threatened to undermine global economic growth and exerted pressure on markets at a time when many countries particularly resource dependant countries like Russia, Brazil and Australia were already struggling. China's move to devalue its currency at best may be seen as distress signal from Beijing indicating to the rest of world that underlying fundamental of its economy were not that strong and are/were much weaker than it was believed to be. Swelling levels of debt, bloated state companies and an overall aversion to market forces are swamping China, threatening to derail its ascent to the ranks of rich countries. Faced with persisting drags on the economy—industrial overcapacity, an overbuilt property market and high corporate debt levels—the leadership has been trying to temper expectations by a public used to high rates of growth.

The bigger issue is in emerging market debt. Commodity focused corporates in Brazil, Russia, India and China that have borrowed in US dollars will face ruin next year (2016). The rising value of the US dollar and collapse of emerging market currencies will make repayments unaffordable for many. The collapse of the junk bond market will reach far and wide. In the past, the junk bond market has only really been used by professional investors or those with a higher risk appetite. As interest rates were cut from 2009 onwards retail investors, pension funds and insurance companies alike have all ploughed billions into high-yield bonds.

Western countries governments and institutional as well as retail investors felt the jolt, due to sharp devaluation of Russian, Indian and Chinese currency and falling stock-markets, due to China's weak economic data in first week of January-2016 itself China stock markets suffered unprecedented losses, massive fall resulted in U.S$2.5 Trillion erosion in market capitalization worldwide, which sent shock waves across global financial markets and all the leading stock markets across the world fell and saw steep decline in valuations. However exact quantum and amount of financial loss suffered has not been reported but it will be safe to assume that many Portfolio investors, Pension funds, hedge funds and investment banks of western countries particularly those from U.S and Britain and also Japanese who all had heavily invested in Indian and China stock markets and also had invested in debt instruments like government bonds have/had suffered monumental financial losses.

So it always makes sense to have well balanced business strategy and always nice to hedge risk, and to have mixed and diversify investment portfolio.

Now there is another perspective, during times when the large Western and Japanese Multinational companies and banks were overwhelmingly interested in India's and China's economic growth prospect and keen to invest money in India and China.

The Chinese made a smart move, China gradually and smartly started growing their trade and commerce with the African countries, also started making investment in Africa in a big way, in 1980 it seems the trade between China and Africa was only U.S$1 Billion, which spectacularly grew to over US$200 Billion by 2014.

Not just China started investing in Africa and increased its trade and commerce with African countries, but China also improved its ties with Latin American (south-America) countries, and have recoded magnificent growth in trade and commerce with Latin American countries, China trade with south-American countries is more than entire European continent countries put together.

The south-American region of the world has grossly been ignored by the rest of the world, not just Latin America offers excellent economic opportunities, but most people in the world don't know one more brutal fact about Latin America that it is arguably the most corrupt and violence prone region of the world. The mainstream western Media is fully focused on Islamic problems and terrorism, the violence and terrorist activities in Islamic countries is prominently reported and extensively covered by western media. The U.S and west-European politicians and government officials only have Arabian problems and India's and China's economic growth prospect on top of their mind, little or no time do these western politicians have to understand the tremendous business and economic growth prospect of Africa particularly west-Africa and more importantly the crimes that occurs in almost every south-American countries. Street corner shootouts, drug trafficking, mafias and criminal gang wars, apart there are rampant incidents of robbery, cheating, kidnappings and killings in south-American cities and countries.

So Latin America has both sides of it, the combination of good and bad, there is positive side of it and negative side of the reality, depends on you, how you perceive things, so ignoring the negative side, let us have positive perspective, we'll discuss **positive aspect** of south-America, South America has lot to offer in terms of business opportunities and lot to see and learn about their Great culture, wonderful people and its glorious history.

Latin America should be a fertile source of business opportunities. Latin America is not only geographically close to U.S but is rich in natural resources, has a relatively young population and possesses political institutions that are becoming increasingly democratic and stable. The conditions appear to be conducive for ample trade and international investment opportunities.

Latin America is made up of countries with commonalities in history and language but also remarkable differences in ethnic makeup, size and cultural traits. Differences also abound in the countries' levels of income and in their investment and commercial relationships with the U.S. and the rest of the world. Understanding these large differences—with the U.S. and among fellow Latin American countries—is vital to understanding the challenges and opportunities for the U.S. south of its border.

China has been seen as an alternative to the United States and Europe by Latin American nations for support in the international community, for funding of infrastructure and humanitarian aid, and for creating economic growth.

The Inter-American Development Bank says Latin America is the next global bread basket. With a third of the world's fresh water resources and more than a quarter of its good quality farmland, this region has everything China needs.

Latin America's trade with China will surpass that of the continent with Europe in two years, according to a United Nations study, with some predicting it will eventually eclipse its trade with the United States. Chinese investment in the continent's energy and infrastructure sectors is rising rapidly, with more than US$550 billion of infrastructure projects in the market.

China's growth in the past decade and its insatiable appetite for commodities has seen resource-rich countries like Brazil prosper. Latin America's largest economy is now the world's biggest exporter of foodstuffs like sugar cane, orange juice and soybean. Much of it is destined for Asia.

Just as Asia is ripe with opportunities for those who have solid business ideas to transplant into the local market, Central America and South America have plenty of opportunities, as well.

However, the Americas are an entirely different marketplace not only in their largely common language but in some of the cultural traits to either appeal to or repel expat entrepreneurs from starting businesses here.

It's a simple equation: fewer people each year are classified as poor and more people are becoming middle class, and consumption is increasing. You can do all the **technical analysis** on emerging markets you want, but GDP growth in some country slipping from 6% to 5.5% isn't going to put the genie back in the bottle.

As we frequently discuss, some of the best opportunities are the ones that already exist in more developed markets. A service that warehouses books and delivers them to your home, eliminating the need for book stores? That doesn't exist in many Latin countries.

This is an oft-repeated claim, usually by Type-A personalities like myself who want things done quickly. Latin America is no Hong Kong, where things are done with laser speed and precision.

In much of Asia, efficiency in the workplace is like a badge of honor. In Malaysia, the ethnic Chinese and Indians frequently complain about the "lazy Malays" who enjoy special benefits. The people complaining ought to come to South America.

You can have an idea to revolutionize an existing business with greater efficiencies, but you need the local staff to help you put your plan in motion.

You need to have Experience which is important, but what is even more important and significant is to have **Judgement**, it is so that many of us make tremendous Judgement errors, all our life we ignore good things and appreciate wrong things. It is good to have excellent Communication skills, but even more important is to have better and more effective **Listen Skills**, most people have appalling listening skills and people with poor listening skills often create problems and misunderstanding for themselves as well for others.

The problems have been institutionalized, to eradicate poverty, we need globally coordinated approach, we need free market trade policies, **Chronic economic and humanitarian aid leads to Chronic problems**. The simple solution is to have more rational Liberal global trade policies, global commerce and trade policies needs to become more rational and unbiased, tariff structure needs to be restructured and be made more simpler with lower tariff and duties on items, easy availability of credit, no particular country should enjoy special privileges and each country should be at Par with other competing nations, so that it enables level playing field to all, Monopolies should be broken.

Frequent "Grants and financial aid packages" provided to the impoverish 3rd world and underdeveloped countries only further aggravates the situation, creates more uncertainty, because it makes governments and their people become more lethargic and loses fighting spirit to meet global challenges. There is no harm in taking or seeking help and support from others in dire circumstances once in a while, but, don't ever make it a habit to live and to survive on others help and support, because it makes a person/persons ever so dependent on others and he/she loses ability to do anything constructive on their own and forever remains dependant on others help and support.

What is urgently needed is to empower the youths and women, provide them access to necessary skills and training so that they become more independent and can manage themselves at work. What is most required, is large amount of money which needs to be allocated for the welfare and benefit of **Senior Citizens**, it is the elder senior citizens who need more care and special attention, so sincere support is required to develop old-age homes for the elders who are alone and suffers extreme health problems, therefore in each country, their government agencies should have volunteers to help safeguard the interest of senior citizens in every possible manner, in every aspect and respect.

Like Latin America another larger part of the world which is West-Africa, W-Africa also provides excellent business opportunities, good for almost every kind of businesses, Service sector, manufacturing sector and agriculture sector, plus affordable low cost labour, high scope to exploit minerals and setting up upstream manufacturing industries to make high-end value added products, large companies and businesses and venture capitalists needs to take risk of making investments in diverse fields and in different parts of the world, countries in Africa and south-America needs massive investments and need technological upgradation, it is needed for global peace and stability, there will be peace in our world only when we create jobs for youngsters,

It is always good to be politically correct, but when Politicians are politically incorrect, than "All hell breaks loose," something that happened in Greece, Greece might have glorious ancient history of gods and goddesses, according to some historians Greece is a birthplace of Western civilization, but 21st century Greek politicians are inept, insipid and ineffective at least that's what they've proved to be, Greece economy plunged into severe crisis sometime in 2010 and it was first sovereign debt crisis in the *Eurozone*, structural weakness, in Greek economy caused sudden crisis of confidence among lenders, in 2012 Greece government had largest **sovereign debt default** in history, and as of 2015 Greece's economy showing no sign of any significant recovering, Greece's citizens have been facing some brutal economic hardship, all because of flawed and faulty economic and political decisions taken by Greece's politicians and country's governing authority, at least on 2 occasions first in 2014 and later in 2015 there was an opportunity for Greece to exit from European union, break all ties with European union and to get rid of the diktat of ECB (*European central bank*) and of IMF (international monetary fund), but for reasons best known to the ruling political dispensation of Greece they preferred to remain with European union and accepted some extremely harsh terms and conditions to secure economic bailout package and money to repay its debt, now it would have made world of sense for the Greeks to break ties with European union and abandon Euro currency, which would have given them opportunity to reintroduce their very own currency **Drachma**, with Greece's own currency, and their own independent monetary and industrial policy, the Greeks then would have succeeded in rebuilding their country, developed their tourism industry and by devaluing their own currency <u>Drachma</u> Greece would potentially have become low cost manufacturing hub in Europe, so had Greece's politicians shown greater maturity and broken ties with European union, there would have been short term initial pain, but over medium to long term Greece citizens would have substantially benefited. Also independence to decide its own political policies would have helped Greece frame its own immigration policy and that would have helped Greece be in a better position to deal with refugee and migrant crisis.

Folks should keep in mind that "Commercial Banks are not humanitarian institutions" but they are lenders, so when a bank lends you money it is also their job to recover money back from you, therefore even while using your Credit Card to make payments at top tier restaurant or in upscale shopping mall, keep it in your mind that you'll also have to pay back money that you spend today, so be within your limits, your reckless spending will make coming generations bankrupt. Lending money is risky business. Even when the borrower pledges a collateral that the lender can confiscate and sell to recover the lent funds, shifts in economic fundamentals can render the loan worthless. The term toxic debt has been used loosely and encompasses a wide variety of loans, but usually refers to mortgages and mortgage-backed loans that became nearly worthless in the first decade of the 21st century.

Article title **"Toxic Loans Around the World Weigh on Global Growth"** explains; "Beneath the surface of the global financial system lurks a multitrillion-dollar problem that could sap the strength of large economies for years to come. The problem is the giant, stagnant pool of loans that companies and people around the world are struggling to pay back. Bad debts have been a drag on economic activity ever since the financial crisis of 2008, but in recent times, the threat posed by an overhang of bad loans appears to be rising. China is the biggest source of worry. Some analysts estimate that China's troubled credit could exceed $5 trillion, a staggering number that is equivalent to half the size of the country's annual economic output.

Official figures show that Chinese banks pulled back on their lending in December-2015. If such trends persist, China's economy, the second-largest in the world behind the United States', may then slow even more than it has, further harming the many countries that have for years relied on China for their growth.

But it's not just China. Wherever governments and central banks unleashed aggressive stimulus policies in recent years, a toxic debt hangover has followed. In the United States, it took many months for mortgage defaults to fall after the most recent housing bust — and energy companies are struggling to pay off the cheap money that they borrowed to pile into the shale (shale oil) boom.

In Europe, analysts say bad loans total more than $1 trillion. Many large European banks are still burdened with defaulted loans, complicating policy makers' efforts to revive the Continent's economy. Italy, for instance, announced a plan last week (of January-2016) to clean out bad loans from its plodding banking industry.

Elsewhere, bad loans are on the rise at Brazil's biggest banks, as the country grapples with the effects of an enormous credit binge."..........

Money-money-money; money arguably is each humans top priority, few people in world have lots of money, but, lots of people in world have less money or no money.

The reasons why there's chaos and troubles in many Muslim ruled countries and in Muslim dominated countries, it is because of economic backwardness, with large Muslim population socially and economically backwards, in Muslim dominated countries like Afghanistan, Pakistan, Bangladesh, Tunisia, Egypt, Somalia and many more countries there is high level of unemployment and or underemployment, big majority of people find it difficult to find jobs, so people have less or no money in their pockets, but at the same time rising prices of essentials are increasing cost of living, day to day expenses are rising but earning opportunities are dwindling.

Religion holds back progress, who has failed whom? "Has their religion (Islam) failed Muslims or Muslim folks have failed their religion?" it is their religion (Islam) that has failed Muslims.

Backwardness no development, no new industrial projects, no plan of new business investments, all is not well in Muslim ruled countries, millions of Muslim families living and surviving in desperate poverty, can't simply blame terrorism and corruption for all the failures in many Muslim ruled countries.

Muslim folks loyalty is only with their religion and not with humanity, people live life to serve purpose of their religion and care less to serve purpose of humanity, callous and arrogant Muslim community but particularly the Sunni Muslim community without any remorse and regrets publically calls every Non- Sunni Muslim religious communities and people as Kafir (infidels) and considers infidels as evil, and Sunni Muslims are of the view that harming infidels in any which manner is their mandated holy duty, Sunnis endeavour is to have this world free of Kafirs (infidels) by any which means possible.

Secular peace loving and liberals considers jihadists elements as terrorists and monsters, but for the Sunni Muslim community those members of their community who joins jihadists group and becomes a jihadi, the Jihadists are considered sacred and for Sunnis whosoever is a jihadi is part of Islamic army and duty of Islamic army is to wipe out all those people and everything in world that is non-Islamic.

It is often debated and discussed at length in public places as well in media, that it is oil money that is funding and aiding Sunni jihadist forces, many political analysts blame and accuses the wealthy oil rich Sunni Arab countries like the Saudis, Qataris and Kuwaitis for funding and financing Sunni extremism and terrorism, it is alleged that most of the Islamic schools and institutions in many different countries are funded by wealthy oil rich Arab countries, and Islamic schools and institutions are perfect breeding ground for radicalization process, young boys and girls are brainwashed, are incited and encouraged to take up Guns and Explosive materials in their hands and do not show any remorse and not to hesitate one bit firing and blasting Non-Sunni Muslim people anywhere in the world so as to fulfil their beloved prophet dream and Islamic god "Allah's" order to establish complete Islamic rule all over the world.

Many medieval Muslim thinkers, overwhelmingly pursue strong Islamist agenda, in mostly Muslim dominated countries young Sunni Muslim boys and girls are prevented from pursuing modern era graduate studies and university studies, schools and institutions in few of the Islamic countries are often brutally attacked, schools and universities in Pakistani city of Peshawar often comes under attack, terrorists brutally killing teachers and students inside schools and universities classrooms.

Insular belief and mind-set as well as rigid attitude, large population not willing to change with times are some of the uncanny reasons for social and economic backwardness and also for political instability in many Muslim countries.

Massive fall in prices of petroleum oil and gas since the middle of year 2014, some political analysts thought and felt will help dent Islamic terrorism because the large oil and gas producing Sunni Arab countries will earn lot less money, crude oil prices falling from the high of $115 per barrel in first half of 2014 to as low as $28 per barrel in January-2016, but on the contrary the Sunni militants and terrorists attacks and activities further increased since 2014, Sunni terrorists vigorously have been targeting and attacking non-Sunni Muslim targets around the world.

Steepest fall in oil prices, oil and gas producing Arab nations are in quandary, because of escalating violence and civil wars in many Islamic countries also because of Islamic sectarian strife, it is difficult to ascertain the fact as in due to massive drop in oil prices if the once cash rich Arabs still have cash dollars in hands or not, whatsoever maybe the truth about Arab's finances, but one thing is evident that due to major disturbance and increased terrorism in Islamic world, the cash rich Arab countries like Saudi Arabia, Qatar and Kuwait are forced to increase their defence budget, squeeze on resources, the Sunni Arab countries but also Shia ruled Iraq have to spend more money buying arms and ammunitions, sharp increases in defence expenditure, all this means that Arabs are earning lot less money but have to spend lot more money on buying arms, food and medicines, plus at same time they also have to take care of their respective country's citizens social security and welfare.

Disastrous fall in prices of petroleum oil and gas has or will force countries like Iraq and Saudi Arabia to borrow more money from international financial markets to finance their increase expenditure, which will increase Arab countries sovereign debt and if oil prices sustains lower levels for longer period of time, in which case all Arab countries will have to drastically reduce subsidies and cut benefits that they've long been providing their citizens and will be compel to raise local taxes, this is fearful situation an imminent risk that increase in taxes on citizens and massive cut in subsidies will further jeopardize the Islamic world and cause more civilian unrest and create political instability. Also because in good times these wealthy Sunni Arab countries Saudi Arabia, Qatar, Kuwait provides large financial aid and grants and financial support to many impoverish Sunni Muslim dominated countries like Pakistan, Bangladesh and North-Sudan etc, if oil revenue falls and income declines in which case Arabs won't be in position to provide prodigious financial support to other chiefly Sunni Muslim countries and will be unable fund various social and religious Islamic institutions.

But it is not that the lower commodity prices will exclusively harm only the Islamic countries, sharp cut in commodities prices will have far reaching consequences, many other resource dependent countries like Venezuela, Brazil and Russia all these countries may experience civilian unrest and social problems which could create sustain political instability, if petroleum oil prices remain low for longer period of time, it potentially might have devastating consequences on world's biggest oil and gas producing and exporting country Russia, with sharp downwards correction in Russian currency (Ruble) against prominent international currencies, weak Russian currency has or will substantially reduce Russians spending and purchasing power, all this uncertainty in commodity markets doesn't augur to well for global stability, painstakingly considering and evaluating every aspect and factors as it is said that 2014/15 commodity crisis is far worse than any other financial crisis that must have been experienced before or in the past.

Weak China's economic data and falling oil prices it was a dreadful start of the year 2016 which started on a chaotic note at least as far as financial markets are concern, the worse start of a new year in history for Capital markets as many trade experts say, all of world's major stock-markets experienced steepest fall ever in first couple of weeks of January-2016, with U.S.A and China's stock-markets suffered the maximum losses. Amid doom there was one positive development which will perhaps add all new dimension to world's economic growth, here I'm talking about lifting of International sanctions on Iran, after successful negotiation, punitive sanctions that were impose on Iran for its alleged Nuclear programme, **United Nations** and **United States of America** lifted most of the crucial Trade embargo and Economic sanctions against Iran in January-2016.

Manufacturing activity is imploding all over the Planet, global trade is slowing that is extremely alarming, the dismal economic numbers continues to stun all of the experts, it is hard pill to swallow. If Chinese economy remains in slump and if there is no dramatic recovery in sight and if China is unable to provide leadership role, so if China fails to pull global economy out of recession than the world community has to look elsewhere, we need someone else to play dominant leadership role, there are prominent markets south-America and Africa, but **Persian nation Iran** in particular has distinct advantage of replacing China and emerge as top performing economy. What does Iran has to offer the world? Iran is exclusive and have many distinct uniqueness which perhaps no other country in world have.

Apart from vast reserves and deposits of petroleum oil and gas and other strategic minerals, as Iran itself is a prominent Shia country, it has advantage of Iraq another largest oil producing country being Iran's neighbour and it further benefits because Iraq also is a Shia ruled country, plus Iran has better connectivity to some of the most lucrative trading route with access to both west-Asia and Central Asia as well easy access to Indian sub-continent countries, also Africa and Europe as well are not far from Iran, apart from geographically situated at strategic location, Iran also has many domestic advantages, it has vibrant manufacturing and services sector, and promising agriculture sector, significant achievements in science and technology, art and culture, fashion and design, tremendous cultural heritage, good scope to attract religious tourism, and also potential to attract large number of art loving and leisure tourists. Besides Iran have large talented pool of people, skilled younger demographic, Iran have secular fashionable and fun loving population and there's no linguistic problems as majority of Iranians speaks multiple languages. **You just ask for it! And the Persians will provide you.**

So if China fails, Iran has all the right attributes to become next economic growth engine and power global economic growth.

But a lot depends on how best Iran can take advantage of the situation and of the vast available natural resources, Iran will have to learn to make optimal use and take maximum advantage of resources, *value is in value addition*, and for that they will have to set up upstream industries and factories to manufacture value added chemicals and petroleum products using domestically available raw material which is of course oil and gas, strengthen its manufacturing and services sector, technological upgradation and modernization of process is needed to add more value to its agriculture sector.

We humans should always keep options open, if one fails try another, success and failure are part and parcel of life.

Don't downgrade your dreams just to fit your reality, upgrade your conviction to make your destiny.

"Common sense is like a deodorant, those who need most, they don't use it."

It is believed according to some scientific research studies that we modern Humans appeared on this planet Earth some 200 Thousand years ago. What makes humans different from animals? No creature is able to create and express humour, not only does humour requires creativity, humour also requires to detach oneself from one's surroundings to see odd, surreal or ironic, humans have ability to observe, describe and appreciate all kinds of beautiful things what nature has created.

We humans make moral judgement and moral choices, our thoughts in this way lifts our thinking to different level and enhances our power of imagination that helps us become creative and to think positively about our desires, human-beings however negotiate conflict through socially created values and codes of conduct.

www.ingramcontent.com/pod-product-compliance
Lightning Source LLC
Chambersburg PA
CBHW070328190526
45169CB00005B/1797